# 100 Library Lifesavers

# 100 Library Lifesavers

## A Survival Guide for School Library Media Specialists

PAMELA S. BACON

2000
Libraries Unlimited, Inc.
Englewood, Colorado

*To Nancy Witty, my mentor and friend.*

Libraries Unlimited, Inc.
P.O. Box 6633
Englewood, CO 80155-6633
1-800-237-6124
www.lu.com

**Library of Congress Cataloging-in-Publication Data**

Bacon, Pamela S., 1964-
    100 library lifesavers : a survival guide for school library media specialists / Pamela S. Bacon.
        p.   cm.
    Includes index.
    ISBN 1-56308-750-2
    1. School libraries--United States.   I. Title.   II. Title: One hundred library lifesavers.
Z675.S3B19      1999
027.8'0973--dc21                                        99-38136
                                                        CIP

# CONTENTS

# LIFESAVER TOOLS SUMMARY

P = Primary
I = Intermediate
E = Elementary
S = Middle/High School
A = All Grades

# LIST OF CONTRIBUTORS

Wendy Auman, Teacher
Walnut Elementary School
R.R. 1
New Ross, IN 47968
Phone: (765) 362-0542
Fax: (765) 362-0545
E-mail: bauman@abcs.com


Tamora K. Brewer, Assistant
    Principal
Tzouanakis Intermediate School
500 Linwood Drive
Greencastle, IN 46135
Phone: (765) 653-4700
Fax: (765) 653-6449
E-mail: tbrewer@greencastle.
    k12.in.us


Toni Buzzeo, Library Media
    Specialist
Longfellow School Library
Portland, ME 04103
E-mail: buzzeocyll@mix-net.net


Pamela Gelbmann, Media
    Generalist
Madison Elementary School
650 Territorial Road NE
Blaine, MN 55434
E-mail: gelbman@ties.k12.mn.us


Randi Hermans, Teacher-
    Librarian
East Chilliwack Elementary
10124 Shamrock Drive
Chilliwack, BC Canada V2P5L4
E-mail: rhermans@chill.org


Joanne Ladewig, Information
    Center Director
Fairgrove Academy
14615 Sauder Street
Valinda, CA 91744
E-mail: shatz@lightside.com


Donna Luther, Media Specialist
Southmore Intermediate
2106 Willowdell
Seabrook, TX 77586
E-mail: dluther@tenet.edu

Sue Maddux, Teacher
Rockville Elementary School
406 W. Elm Street
Rockville, IN 47872
Phone: (765) 569-5363
E-mail: smaddux@rockville.k12.in.us

SPLC (Student Press Law Center)
1101 Wilson Boulevard
Suite 1910
Arlington, VA 22209
Phone: (703) 807-1904
E-mail: splc@splc.org

Nancy Witty, Media Specialist
Rockville Elementary School
406 W. Elm Street
Rockville, IN 47872
Phone: (765) 569-5363
E-mail: nwitty@rockville.k12.in.us

# ACKNOWLEDGMENTS

Many of the ideas in this book came as a direct result of my years as a traveling librarian. I am no longer forced to travel between schools, but when I did, I knew it was critical for me to develop time-saving techniques and tools to survive in the sea of to-do lists floating around me. One of my biggest lifesavers was my friend and colleague, Nancy Witty. Nancy is a dedicated professional whose creativity never fails to amaze and inspire me. Another lifesaver was my high school friend and graphic designer, Holly Cartwright. Holly's help was a lifesaver in more ways than one! Last, to my family and friends, who were there to keep me afloat while I wrote this book, thank you!

# INTRODUCTION

*100 Library Lifesavers: A Survival Guide for School Library Media Specialists* was created especially for busy school librarians. The book includes *tips* (author's suggestions), *tools* (ready-to-use lifesavers), and *talk* (quotes from practicing media specialists) to help you stay afloat. Throughout the book, the terms *librarian* and *media specialist* are used interchangeably. Although I personally believe the word *librarian* has a warmer connotation, I have alternated it with *media specialist* as it sounds more professional. No matter which title you prefer, I hope this book helps you find more time to model your love of reading, which, I believe, binds us together under any name.

# THE STORY ON INVENTORY

If the word *inventory* makes you shudder, have no fear! The Ongoing Inventory Chart (Lifesaver Tool 1.1) will help you put those fears in order—literally! This inventory method allows you to set your own pace. Inventory is completed throughout the year in small segments, rather than at the year's end as in more traditional methods. Although not a perfect system, this method allows me to keep a handle on three different library inventories. This method may not work for everyone, but it certainly gives me time at the end of the year to track down overdues and, believe it or not, even do some much needed weeding!

## Lifesaver Tips

- The Ongoing Inventory Chart is broken into segments. If this schedule is not manageable for your needs, make any needed adjustments.

- For those of you who are compulsive (like me!), this method may feel uncomfortable at first, but give it a try!

- If you get behind on your schedule, do two sections the following week.

- Instead of writing on your shelflist card, I suggest you attach a red paper clip to the card. The next year, use a paper clip of a different color. By color coding, you can easily keep track of how many years the book has been missing and act accordingly. You save time, too, because you are no longer forced to remove a shelflist card and manually record the year each time a book is missing.

- If time allows, and you choose to do so, you can go through the cards with red clips only at the end of the year.

- The idea is that even if a card contains a red clip, chances are the book was simply in circulation during inventory. If this is the case, the next school year you will automatically catch the book in its place on the shelf.

- If a book is missing three years in a row, it's a good bet the book is either on permanent loan or gone forever! The colored clips and shelflist cards can then be removed from your collection files.

 Before completing year-end inventory, enlist the support of your administration to have overdue books returned. Our school, for example, won't let students attend field fun day if they have outstanding books.

Tamora K. Brewer,
Assistant Principal, Tzouanakis
Intermediate School, Greencastle, IN

# ONGOING INVENTORY CHART

| Section | To Be Done | Date Done | Initials |
|---|---|---|---|
| Fiction A–B | Week 1 | | |
| Fiction C | Week 2 | | |
| Fiction D–E | Week 3 | | |
| Fiction F–G | Week 4 | | |
| Fiction H | Week 5 | | |
| Fiction I–J | Week 6 | | |
| Fiction K–L | Week 7 | | |
| Fiction M | Week 8 | | |
| Fiction N–O | Week 9 | | |
| Fiction P | Week 10 | | |
| Fiction Q–R | Week 11 | | |
| Fiction S | Week 12 | | |
| Fiction T–U | Week 13 | | |
| Fiction V–W | Week 14 | | |
| Fiction X–Z | Week 15 | | |
| 000–099 | Week 16 | | |
| 100–199 | Week 17 | | |
| 200–299 | Week 18 | | |
| 300–399 | Week 19 | | |
| 400–499 | Week 20 | | |
| 500–599 | Week 21 | | |
| 600–699 | Week 22 | | |
| 700–799 | Week 23 | | |
| 800–899 | Week 24 | | |
| 900–999 | Week 25 | | |
| Biographies | Week 26 | | |
| Magazines | Week 27 | | |
| Paperbacks | Week 28 | | |

**Lifesaver Tool 1.1.** **Ongoing Inventory Chart**

# PASS THE BUCK

When I began using Book Bucks, I had no idea how the idea would pay off (no pun intended!). Not only are Book Bucks a wonderful way to motivate students to read, this token system is also a powerful behavior modification tool.

## Lifesaver Tips

- Photocopy and laminate a good supply of Book Bucks (Lifesaver Tool 2.1. Sample Book Bucks) at the beginning of the school year. Because they'll last a long time, you won't need to make as many in subsequent years. For counterfeiting purposes (this has happened with junior high students!), I also mark the back of each Book Buck (before laminating) with a special library stamp.

- Give Book Bucks when students return books on time.

- Give Book Bucks when students win library contests or contribute at library class.

- Allow students to buy prizes with Book Bucks. For example, you might charge 3 Book Bucks for a bookmark; 5 Book Bucks for a pencil; 10 Book Bucks for candy; or 25 Book Bucks for a book to keep.

- I strongly suggest adopting my philosophy: If I give Book Bucks, I can also take them away!

- Allowing students to use Book Bucks to purchase a bean-bag chair or a special seat during library class is also effective.

- Troll bonus points are a nice way to fund books that students can buy with Book Bucks.

- You might allow students to use Book Bucks during the book fair instead of real money—parents really appreciate this idea and students learn the value of money at the same time!

  *Note*: Keep in mind that if you allow students to purchase books with Book Bucks, you will not be able to keep as many books for the library. Basically, you trade any book fair profits for free books and other incentives instead of accepting the cash option. Because this means you don't keep as many books for the library, I usually hold two book fairs per year. Students can use Book Bucks at only one of the fairs; the library keeps all books and/or profits from the other fair.

- To make purchasing items with Book Bucks simpler, copy the following Book Bucks Order Form, which students fill out on their own and turn in. (Lifesaver Tool 2.2. Book Bucks Order Form)

 Wondering how to stretch your library budget? Read *The Dollar Stretcher* at http://www.stretcher.com.

Pamela Bacon

# BOOK BUCKS

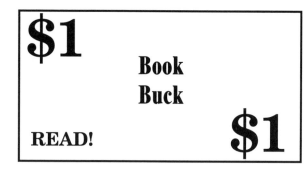

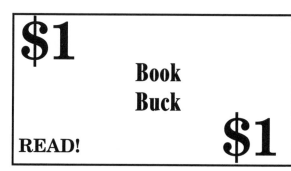

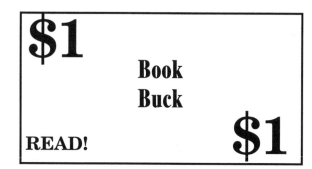

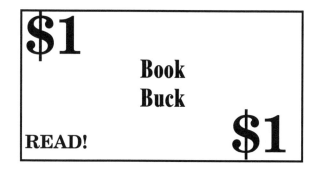

<u>**Lifesaver Tool 2.1.**</u>   **Sample Book Bucks**

# BOOK BUCKS ORDER FORM

Name_____ Teacher_____

Directions:

1.  Write your name and your teacher's name above.

2.  Circle the items below that you wish to purchase.

3.  Paper-clip your Book Bucks to this form.

4.  The item(s) purchased will be delivered as soon as possible!

| Item | Price |
|------|-------|
| Bookmark | $3 |
| Pencil | $5 |
| Candy | $10 |
| Paperback Book | $25 |
| Other Items As Announced! | ? |

**Lifesaver Tool 2.2.**   **Book Bucks Order Form**

# GOING ONCE, GOING TWICE...

I must give full credit to my twin sister for this lifesaver; she came up with the idea of a Silent Auction—and the students are sure sold on it!

## Lifesaver Tips

- Suggested grade levels: Grades 4–8.

- Designate a special spot in the media center for Silent Auction items.

- At the beginning of each month, put out three new Silent Auction items on which the students can "bid" using their Book Bucks.

- Any item can be a Silent Auction item—as long as the students will bid!

- Big-ticket item ideas—fast-food lunches, posters, Cokes and popcorn, paperback books, and highlighters. The possibilities are endless!

- Students fill out a Silent Auction Form (Lifesaver Tool 3.1) and drop it into a ballot box.

- At the end of each month, award the items to the highest bidders.

- Once the students get used to the format, the program virtually runs itself.

- At the beginning of each school year, photocopy lots of Silent Auction Forms—you'll need them!

IIII➡ Watch out for counterfeit Book Bucks!

Pamela Bacon

# SILENT AUCTION FORM

Name_____

Teacher_____

What item(s) do you want to buy?          Your bid:

_____          $ _____

_____          $ _____

_____          $ _____

_____          $ _____

_____          $ _____

_____          $ _____

Notes:

- Don't turn in your Book Bucks with your bid—I'll collect later!
- If you bid, make sure you have enough Book Bucks!

Prizes will be delivered on:

Monday

Tuesday

Wednesday

Thursday

Friday

**Lifesaver Tool 3.1.   Silent Auction Form**

# PLAN ON GOOD BEHAVIOR!

As you know, discipline can sometimes be a problem for "special" teachers! Because there are no grades to hold over their heads, students may not always take library class seriously. In addition, because you see the child only on a weekly basis, it is often hard to develop a positive student-teacher relationship, especially with the more challenging students! Because of these limitations, I have designed an individual plan that works for me. I use this plan for severe or ongoing discipline problems. I hope you'll never need to use this one, but here it is!

## Lifesaver Tips

- Be sure to obtain signatures from the classroom teacher and the principal before using the L.I.B. (Library Individual Behavior) Plan (Lifesaver Tool 4.1) and the Follow-Up Note Form (Lifesaver Tool 4.2).

- Be sure to have individual assignment folders, containing high-quality library lessons, ready at all times. When a child misbehaves, this is not the time to search for an appropriate assignment.

- This plan has worked for some of my most severe behavior problems.

- Because the student is no longer receiving the desired attention from the class, poor behavior usually ceases immediately upon isolation.

- When the child's behavior improves enough that he or she can be removed from the plan, just the threat of re-implementing the plan often improves behavior!

- Behavior of classmates improves when they see that an organized plan is ready should they choose to exhibit poor library behavior!

 Need a little discipline? Enroll in one of Lee Canter's independent study courses (1-800-669-9011). Earn three graduate credit hours right from the comfort of your own home—if you're not too undisciplined!

Pamela Bacon

# L.I.B. (LIBRARY INDIVIDUAL BEHAVIOR) PLAN

Because of continued unacceptable behavior, your child has been placed on an Individual Behavior Plan in library class.

Here is how the plan works:

- Each week a note will be sent home regarding your child's progress.

- If your child returns the signed note at the beginning of the next class, your child may participate in the activities with the rest of the class.

- If the note is not signed and returned, the child will automatically go to an assigned seat in isolation. Be advised, your child will still receive a library lesson and, if earned, the chance to check out materials.

- If your child chooses to disrupt while in isolation, an after-school detention or visit to the principal may be assigned. Be sure to check your child's note for information.

If your child behaves appropriately:

- Book Bucks will be earned.

- Your child may check out materials.

- Your child will regain participation in fun learning activities with the rest of the class.

The L.I.B. Plan is designed to improve your child's behavior by giving immediate consequences and rewards based on his or her choices. I believe your child will benefit from this structured plan. Thank you for your support!

_____          _____
Student's Signature                              Parent's Signature


_____          _____
Librarian's Signature                            Principal's Signature


_____          _____
Teacher's Signature                              Date

**Lifesaver Tool 4.1.   L.I.B. (Library Individual Behavior) Plan**

# L.I.B. (LIBRARY INDIVIDUAL BEHAVIOR) PLAN
# FOLLOW-UP NOTE

Dear _____:

    Just a follow-up note on your child's progress/behavior in the library!

Please feel free to call me at _____ if you have any questions. Thank you for your support!

\_\_\_\_\_Your child returned the note and was well behaved!

\_\_\_\_\_Your child returned the note, but was disruptive.

    \_\_\_\_\_ Your child was sent to isolation during library class.

    \_\_\_\_\_ Your child disrupted class while in isolation.

    \_\_\_\_\_ Your child was assigned an after-school detention on

    _____(date and time).

    \_\_\_\_\_ Your child was sent to the principal's office.

    \_\_\_\_\_ Your child was not allowed to check out materials.

Comments:

_____

_____

_____

Sincerely,

_____

Media Specialist

Date: _____

**Lifesaver Tool 4.2.**   **Follow-Up Note Form**

# CHECK THIS OUT!

I'm one of the few media specialists who have gone from an automated media center to a nonautomated media center (yes, there are still some around!). When I was online, however, I found there were times when I wanted students to check out books, but that I simply could not be tied to a computer to key in the books at that exact time. You know the story—you're in the middle of helping a student choose books and, suddenly, time is up and you need to be at the computer checking out books. Because we can't be in two places at once (although we try), I started using this Library Checkout Form (Lifesaver Tool 5.1). I then stumbled upon a great idea by putting pictures of books on the form. By changing the books on the form occasionally, students are indirectly exposed to new books. In fact, students often request the spotlighted book. I can now circulate around the library to assist students, monitor behavior, and talk with teachers without being stuck behind the computer. When students leave the media center, I gather forms and enter the books into the computer. This proactive plan allows me to be more in control of my time.

## Lifesaver Tips

- Use this tip only with older students unless you have student helpers or a library aide to write down accession numbers for the primary students.

- Try not to get behind on entering books into the computer (a lesson I've learned the hard way!).

- Even older students need a lot of practice with accession numbers before beginning this plan.

- Run off the form in bright colors to make it more eye-catching.

- When a student completes the form incorrectly, follow up immediately to prevent future errors.

- Change pictures of books on the form monthly to showcase new or seasonal books.

---

 *Never* bother to catalog an item you don't really want as part of your permanent library collection. Students won't check the book out and it's a waste of your precious time.

Pamela Bacon

---

# LIBRARY CHECKOUT FORM

Name_____ Library Number_____

Grade_____ Teacher Homeroom_____

Title of Book _____

Author _____

Accession/Barcode Number _____

Circle One Below!

_____ Checkout

_____ Reserve

_____ Renew

Comments:

_____

_____

_____

_____

_____

From *100 Library Lifesavers.* © 1999 Libraries Unlimited. (800) 237-6124.

**Lifesaver Tool 5.1.   Library Checkout Form**

# SURF'S UP!

With the growing number of teachers, media specialists, and administrators using the Internet, why not have some recommendation forms near the checkout desk?

## Lifesaver Tips

- Keep a binder handy with completed Internet site forms. This creates a wonderful Internet resource tool. (Lifesaver Tool 6.1. Internet Site Form)

- Organize the binder by subjects for ease of use.

- Photocopy forms and distribute to interested teachers.

- The binder could easily be checked out of the professional section of your library.

- This strategy could be used with students, as long as the media specialist previews all sites before putting them in the binder.

 If you need a life net before you surf the Internet, enroll in a noncredit course. Most colleges offer Internet classes for a nominal fee. That way, you can get your feet wet before you surf in front of your students!

Pamela Bacon

# CHECK OUT THIS INTERNET SITE!

Address _____

Title/Home Page _____

Name _____

Subject _____

Comments _____

_____

_____

_____

# CHECK OUT THIS INTERNET SITE!

Address _____

Title/Home Page _____

Name _____

Subject _____

Comments _____

_____

_____

_____

**Lifesaver Tool 6.1.   Internet Site Form**

# LIBRARY MANAGEMENT TIPS

## Lifesaver Tips

- **It's in the cards!** If you've never had students card their own books, try it and see if you like it. When students come into my library, they automatically go to the carpeted area and sit in a circle. Rather than keeping cards behind the date they are due, I keep all the cards behind the teacher's name. Although they can be alphabetized, it is not essential for this procedure. At the beginning of each class, I pull the cards from behind the teacher's name and begin reading them off. The students are taught to 1) match the book with the card; 2) card the book; and 3) turn the book face down (to show that it has been carded). Books left face up at the end of the procedure are those books that were never checked out properly. This strategy therefore reinforces the need for all students to check out books properly. Although a time-consuming procedure, asking for information about each book (author, title, subject, call number, interesting detail, etc.) gives each student a chance to be recognized and a brief opportunity to share information. Also, it's an excellent way to find out immediately which students forgot their books; thus, library skills are reinforced. Although the student will receive an overdue form later, the immediate verbal reminder is effective. What started out as a time-saver quickly became a lifesaver!

- **Forget frustration—say organization!** I bought a simple white basket from DEMCO and asked my husband, a welder, to add wheels (any welding shop performs these types of procedures at a minimal charge) because the rolling basket is wonderful for traveling between schools. Since then, I've seen rolling baskets at a variety of office supply and discount stores. I also purchased three totes in different colors—blue, green, and brown. These totes fit perfectly into the rolling basket. When not in use, the baskets stay in the back of my vehicle. That way, if a teacher from a different building has a request for materials from another library, I simply put the note into the basket of the appropriate color. By using this color-coded system, I rarely forget to follow up because I have the reminder at my fingertips. I've also found I've never lost anything because of a little extra organization.

- **You can only do so much!** I learned this tip the hard way. During my first year as a traveling librarian, I attempted to fill three full-time positions. I held six book fairs (two at each school), attended three back-to-school nights, three open house nights, and three monthly staff meetings—among other scheduled events. Obviously, I found this schedule completely unmanageable and was soon forced to make changes. If the school board refused to hire a full-time professional for each facility, I knew no situation would be ideal. Rather, the best solution for me was to make one of my three schools a base school. At my base school, I attended all functions and teachers' meetings. At my nonbase schools, I was there to fulfill my first priority—provide the best library instruction possible to students! Although this new plan helped tremendously, I must caution that many teachers at my nonbase schools were not pleased with this system. Teachers understandably want a full-time media specialist at their own school and will often make unreasonable demands. When teachers become upset, I try to redirect their energies into advocating for a full-time media specialist in each building.

- **Paper clips, paper clips!** I use color-coded paper clips constantly! As I card books with students (see **It's in the cards!**), I add a paper clip to the card each time the book becomes overdue. By doing this, I can see at a glance how many books are overdue. When a book has two clips (two weeks overdue), I attach a red clip to the card to remind myself to send an overdue notice home (the first two go to the classroom). This is also a visual reminder to myself that the student may not check out materials until he or she has returned the red-clipped item.

To save time, take advantage of Follett's Free Order Typing Service (1-800-435-6170). You can write down a book title on anything from a notebook to a napkin. Send in your scribbles and receive a neatly typed purchase order complete with all information. You don't even have to make a copy before you send the order—they do it for you!

Pamela Bacon

# Five Lifesavers for the
# Traveling Library Media Specialist

**Learn to Say No!**

**Attend Time Management Workshops!**

**Simplify, Simplify, Simplify!**

**Decorate with a Theme That Can Stay Up All Year!**
(Come in and "Sea" Our Books! with an ocean theme is one of my favorites!)

**Invest in a Laptop Computer!**

**Lifesaver Tool 7.1.** **Five Lifesavers for the Traveling Library Media Specialist**

# YOU CAN COUNT ON IT!

After being guilt-ridden for an entire school year, I finally came up with a manageable system to keep track of circulation records. Although I knew it would be impossible to carry out, implement, and maintain a traditional circulation count, I knew I needed some type of circulation records both to show me the strengths (and weaknesses) of my collection and to include in my annual report. Thus, the Random Circulation Count idea was born!

## Lifesaver Tips

- Each month, my library assistant counts and records the number of items checked out for both teachers and students.

- If desired, the count can be broken down into fiction, nonfiction, etc. I found I did not need to be that specific for an elementary media center.

- I pick the first week of the month to perform my circulation count. You could easily choose any other week of the month—whenever works best for your schedule.

- Although this system is random, I feel it is fairly reliable for measuring the number of items checked out and approximate library usage.

• This form is also useful to compare the counts of different media center facilities.

*Note*: The system described above is for use in nonautomated libraries. The attached Lifesaver Tool 8.1 (Random Circulation Count Form), however, could be used in either automated or nonautomated facilities.

 Include your total library circulation count in your annual report. You might want to include numbers from the last five years to show your administration just how much they count on you!

Pamela Bacon

# RANDOM CIRCULATION COUNT

Month: _____ Date: _____

Number of Checkouts:

Students_____ TOTAL (ALL GRADES)

Grade   K_____

Grade   1_____

Grade   2_____

Grade   3_____

Grade   4_____

Grade   5_____

Grade   6_____

Grade   7_____

Grade   8_____

Grade   9_____

Grade 10_____

Grade 11_____

Grade 12_____

Teachers_____

Overdues_____

Completed by: _____(Signature)

**Lifesaver Tool 8.1.   Random Circulation Count Form**

# MEET OVERDUE, THE LIBRARY GHOST!

This lesson plan for intermediate grades can be used any month of the year, but is especially good for October!

## Objectives:

1.  Students will gain proficiency in using card catalog.

2.  Students will match call numbers with correct titles.

3.  Students will practice locating books on shelves.

## Materials Needed:

- Overdue, the Library Ghost handouts. (Lifesaver Tool 9.1. Library Ghost Handout)

- pencils

- card catalog

**Procedures:**

- Pass a handout to each student.

- Tell students they will be using the card catalog to find ghost stories and other scary books.

- Students write the title of the chosen book on the top half of the ghost.

- Students write the corresponding call number on the bottom half of the ghost.

- After the ghost is completed, students go to shelf to locate the chosen book.

- Students may color the ghosts during extra time.

## Lifesaver Tips

- Brainstorm a list of words other than *ghost* so that students won't congregate in the same section!

- For an additional activity, ghosts could be cut apart and older students could try to match the correct top of the ghost (title) and bottom (call number).

 Now that you've talked about ghosts, how about a little mystery? Hold up a badly damaged book. Read aloud a letter from the book (which you've written) describing the horrible things this book has been through. Then hold up other damaged books and ask students to try to solve the mystery for each one.

Pamela Bacon

# OVERDUE, THE LIBRARY GHOST

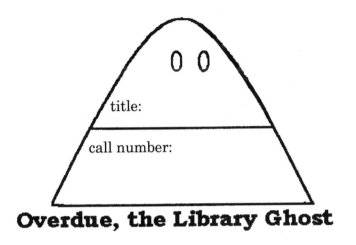

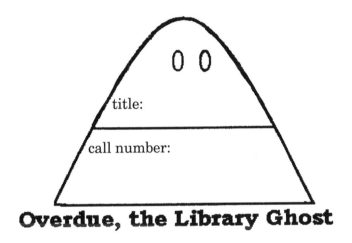

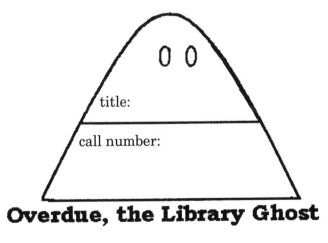

**Lifesaver Tool 9.1.** Library Ghost Handout

# PAM'S PICKS

Because of the budget crunches affecting our schools and libraries, you can't be too careful when selecting library materials. All too often, the media specialist's dwindling dollars are spent on resources that turn out to be disappointing. Here are 10 resources that are worth a million, but don't cost nearly that much! (Lifesaver Tool 10.1. Pam's Picks—A Checklist)

## Lifesaver Tips

- If you don't have money in your budget to purchase new materials, don't be pressured into meeting with a sales representative. It would be a waste of your time (and theirs).

- If you purchase a resource book and are not pleased, return it right away. The longer you keep the item, the less chance you'll have for a refund.

- If you find a valuable resource, e-mail your fellow colleagues. They may not know about it.

- When time allows, meet with other local media specialists. A monthly gathering for dinner could become a great way to find out about new resources.

 Make sure you have a copy of *Recommended Reference Books for Small and Medium-sized Libraries and Media Centers* by Bohdan Wynar (editor) on hand. It's an invaluable source of reviews to check out before you purchase expensive resources.

Pamela Bacon

# PAM'S PICKS—A CHECKLIST

_____ *Hooked on Library Skills: A Sequential Activities Program for Grades K–6* (Marguerite Lewis and P. Kudla)
>Publisher: Center for Applied Research in Education
>Price: $27.95
>*Hooked on Library Skills* includes dozens of activities, challenges and puzzles to make learning important library skills fun and exciting. Best of all, it's designed to meet the needs of every grade level. This book is a must for school librarians!

_____ *How to Use an Almanac* (Video and Fun in Finding Facts kit)
>Publisher: World Almanac Education
>Price: $109.00 (kit); $24.95 (video)
>This kit is a wonderful tool to introduce upper-elementary and middle school students to the world of materials and information that can be found in the almanac. The videotape highlights students searching for a topic and showing step-by-step procedures on how they located their information. This kit also comes with handouts and activities to further emphasize the skills. It even includes a set of 10 almanacs, which will immediately be in great demand!

_____ *Instant Art Notebook*
>Publisher: Linworth
>Price: $34.95
>This resource is dynamite! It includes clip art for every occasion. You'll want to keep this one locked up—it's sure to disappear once teachers see it!

_____ *The Internet for Newbies: An Easy Access Guide* (Constance D. Williams)
>Publisher: Libraries Unlimited
>Price: $20.00
>A practical, comprehensive guide for beginning Internet users.

_____ *The Internet Resource Directory for K–12 Teachers and Librarians* (Elizabeth B. Miller)
>Publisher: Libraries Unlimited
>Price: $27.50
>This book includes current, accurate, useful information about the information superhighway. It includes everything from getting online to using the Internet with students. Wait no longer—hop on the surfboard to curriculum connections and Internet adventure!

_____*School Library Management Notebook* (Catherine M. Andronik)
> Publisher: Linworth
> Price: $36.95
> This indispensable book is full of management tips, organizational tools, public relations, and more.

_____*Secondary School Librarian's Survival Guide* (Jane E. Streiff)
> Publisher: Center for Applied Research in Education
> Price: $32.95
> Ready-to-use techniques, tools, and materials guaranteed to help you save time and work in every aspect of your job as a library media specialist.

_____*Self-Directing Library and Media Center Skills*
> Publisher: Weber Costello
> This book is out of print, but if you can find an old copy, I guarantee you it's priceless!

_____*So You're Going to Run a Library: A Library Management Primer* (Dave Sutton)
> Publisher: Libraries Unlimited
> Price: $22.50
> A how-to guide offering simple, straightforward advice on managing a library facility.

_____*Tips and Other Bright Ideas for School Librarians*
> Publisher: Linworth
> Price: $24.95
> This source includes more than 1,200 tips and ideas to help manage your school library media center. Ideas are easy to use and are field-tested!

**Lifesaver Tool 10.1.   Pam's Picks—A Checklist**

# NEED ASSISTANT ASSISTANCE?

With three different library assistants and three different library assistants' schedules, I needed to come up with a consistent way to communicate my goals and expectations to each aide. Obviously, this form won't fit every situation, but the basic format is provided for you. As you can see, the form provides a place for two-way communications and feedback. This lifesaving tool is especially helpful when a new assistant comes on board. The notebook can be used as a weekly checklist and I can follow up at my convenience. Because the materials are kept in a three-ring binder, I can easily revise or update information.

## Lifesaver Tips

- The following Lifesaver Tool 11.1 (Library Assistant's Notebook Form) is very basic and is designed to work in many of your libraries.

- I also have detailed procedures (e.g., teachers' checkouts, students' checkouts, overdues, etc.) typed and placed in both the Library Assistant's Notebook and my emergency substitute file.

- Be positive when introducing this to your library assistant (especially one who has been around a while). Stress the benefits of a structured list!

 Take your assistant with you to conferences whenever you can!

Pamela Bacon

# LIBRARY ASSISTANT'S NOTEBOOK

Duties for the week of _____.

A.  WEEKLY

_____  1.  Card all books turned in.

_____  2.  Shelve all books.

_____  3.  Assist students during busy library times.

_____  4.  Do ongoing inventory (see schedule).

_____  5.  Check number of copies in folders and run off as necessary
(Silent Auction Forms, Book Bucks Order Forms, Book Bucks, etc.).

_____  6.  Other:


B.  MONTHLY

_____  1.  Calculate Random Circulation Count.

_____  2.  Change bulletin board(s).

_____  3.  Other:


C.  LIBRARY ASSISTANT'S COMMENTS:


D.  LIBRARY MEDIA SPECIALIST'S COMMENTS:


**Lifesaver Tool 11.1.   Library Assistant's Notebook Form**

# MAKING PROGRESS

I have found this strategy extremely beneficial. Although no grades appear on these progress reports and notes to parents, they are an excellent form of feedback for the student, for the teacher, and, perhaps most important, for the parent. Keeping in touch with parents is an extremely powerful technique—whether you're discussing discipline or Dewey! (Lifesaver Tool 12.1. Library Progress Report Form; Lifesaver Tool 12.2. Note to Parents Form)

## Lifesaver Tips

- Be positive when presenting this new idea to students!

- Expect to receive more parent contact with this system (which has its positives and negatives!).

- Following up with parents immediately shows that you are committed to this system.

- Be sure to obtain the principal's approval and the teacher's support before using.

 To encourage a positive response about progress reports, allow the first 10 students to return their signed reports to check out an extra book!

Pamela Bacon

# LIBRARY PROGRESS REPORT

Name_____

Teacher_____ Grade_____

      \_\_\_\_\_ Completed library projects

      \_\_\_\_\_ Reading interest

      \_\_\_\_\_ Computer quizzes

      \_\_\_\_\_ Mastered library research skills

      \_\_\_\_\_ Library behavior

S = Satisfactory

U = Unsatisfactory

N = Needs improvement

E = Excellent

Librarian's Comments:

Parent's Comments:

Student's Signature: _____

Librarian's Signature: _____

Parent's Signature: _____

**Lifesaver Tool 12.1.   Library Progress Report Form**

# FROM THE LIBRARY!

Date: _____

Dear Parents:

You will be receiving library progress reports each _____. This report will let you know how your child is doing in such areas as reading comprehension, research skills, and library behavior.

Because reading for information and enjoyment is so important, I hope this progress report might be helpful to focus the older students on reading before they move on to high school.

There is a place on the progress report for both the librarian and parent to give feedback and suggestions.

Please sign and return the form when you receive it. If you have any questions, I may be reached at _____. The best time to call is _____.

Thank you in advance for your support and cooperation.

Sincerely,

_____
Media Specialist

**Lifesaver Tool 12.2.** **Note to Parents Form**

# A QUICK OBSERVATION

In the library, many times a principal or assistant principal visits informally to ask a question or gain information. Because I wanted to take advantage of these quick impromptu visits, I designed the Informal Evaluation Form (Lifesaver Tool 13.1) so that my administrators can quickly assess the wonderful things going on in the library!

## Lifesaver Tips

- If you wish, this form can also be filled out by teachers (for additional information).

- Until the system becomes more routine, you may need to prompt your administrator by providing the form when he or she visits the library.

- This form is certainly not meant to imply that the administrator should evaluate every time he or she enters the library, but rather this procedure simply provides an informal, alternative way to gain additional evaluation information.

Looking for a way to improve organization when traveling between schools? Use a plastic milk crate attached to a luggage cart to haul items. The crate will hold hanging files, books, supplies, and more. The cart makes it possible to travel between buildings without wrecking your back or having to make multiple trips. I even plop my laptop on top!

Pamela Gelbmann, Media Generalist,
Madison Elementary School, Blaine, MN

# INFORMAL EVALUATION FORM

_____ Students were focused and on task.

_____ Library atmosphere was calm, warm, and inviting.

_____ Library was uncluttered and organized.

_____ Media specialist appeared organized and efficient.

_____ Students' questions were answered quickly.

_____ Communication with teachers/administrators was efficient and professional.

A = Above expectations      M = Meets expectations

B = Below expectations      N = Not observed

Observer's Comments:

Media Specialist's Comments:

**Lifesaver Tool 13.1.   Informal Evaluation Form**

# TIME TO RE-EVALUATE

During my career as a library media specialist, I have never been evaluated on any form other than a standard teacher's evaluation form. Although I do consider myself a teacher first and media specialist second, I feel strongly that many other areas should be considered when evaluating the media specialist. Organization, communication with administrators and staff, and budgetary management are just a few of the items that should be considered during an evaluation.

## Lifesaver Tips

- It may take time to persuade your principal to buy into this new form. Just be patient and keep trying! (Lifesaver Tool 14.1. Media Specialist Evaluation Form)

- In some cases, the school board must approve evaluation criteria.

- There may be additional areas in which you would like to be evaluated; if so, the form can easily be revised.

 Does your principal have a good sense of humor? The next time you're observed, read aloud one of these funny principal stories: *Fabulous Principal Pie* by Jim Hoffman; *The Jellybean Principal* by Catherine McMorrow; and *Don't Go to the Principal's Office* by M. T. Coffin.

Pamela Bacon

# MEDIA SPECIALIST EVALUATION FORM

M = Meets expectations      E = Exceeds expectations

B = Below expectations

## INSTRUCTIONAL

_____ Students observed were on task.

_____ Students' behavior was managed effectively.

_____ Questions were answered quickly and efficiently.

_____ A good relationship with students was observed.

_____ Collaboration/team teaching with teachers was effective.

## ADMINISTRATIVE

_____ Media center was organized and functional.

_____ Student assistants were on task.

_____ Library aide/adult volunteers were on task.

_____ Budget materials appeared well organized.

## PROFESSIONAL

_____ Good communication exists with staff.

_____ Good communication is shown with administration.

_____ The media specialist serves on technology and/or curriculum committee(s).

_____ The media specialist sponsors, attends, or promotes extracurricular activities.

Evaluator's Comments:             Media Specialist's Comments:

_____      _____

Media Specialist              Date

_____      _____

Evaluator/Administrator        Date

**Lifesaver Tool 14.1.**    **Media Specialist Evaluation Form**

# YOU'RE IN JEOPARDY!

Well, actually *you* aren't in jeopardy, but your students will be when they play this fun game that reinforces library skills! Best of all, this Jeopardy activity can be adapted for review on any subject. In addition, it can be played for five minutes or five hours! (Lifesaver Tool 15.1. Library Jeopardy Questions)

## Lifesaver Tips

### Preparation

1. Write each Jeopardy question on separate 4-x-6-inch index cards (write the question on the front and the answer on the back).

2. On the front of each card, write the category and number (e.g., AUTHOR 1).

3. Put the index cards in numerical and category order.

4. Make an index card giving the name of the category.

5. Put this category card on top and rubber-band the cards together (laminate cards, if desired).

6. Using a chalkboard, overhead screen, or dry erase board, make up the following scoreboard (see table 15.1) with five columns across, six rows down.

**Table 15.1  Jeopardy Scoreboard**

| AUTHOR | READING | DEWEY | CARD CAT | POTPOURRI |
|--------|---------|-------|----------|-----------|
| 1 | 1 | 1 | 1 | 1 |
| 2 | 2 | 2 | 2 | 2 |
| 3 | 3 | 3 | 3 | 3 |
| 4 | 4 | 4 | 4 | 4 |
| 5 | 5 | 5 | 5 | 5 |
| 6 | 6 | 6 | 6 | 6 |

*Note*: I have included an extra row for column titles, which you may also wish to do!

## Playing the Game!

- Break up students into teams—groups of four or five are best.

- Assign one student helper to stand in front and put an "X" through used categories.

- Choose a captain for each team.

- Decide which team goes first. Ask that team captain to choose a category and number.

- Begin asking Jeopardy questions from cards.

- After you read a question, put the card face down so that you know it's a dead card.

- After a team chooses a question, the student helper marks an "X" on the board.

- The student helper can also keep score—score is based on the chosen question. For example, for the Category of Reading, question three is worth three points.

- The group with the highest score (either after a set time *or* when all questions have been asked) wins!

- I recommend deducting points from groups who become too loud!

 Let your students be "board!" After playing Jeopardy, try playing other educational board games like Monopoly, Boggle, checkers, and chess on special days.

Pamela Bacon

# LIBRARY JEOPARDY QUESTIONS

CATEGORIES:

| | |
|---|---|
| Author | A |
| Reading | R |
| Card Catalog | CC |
| Dewey | D |
| Potpourri | P |

A 1   Q:   What is another name for Samuel L. Clemens?

     A:   Mark Twain

A 2   Q:   Who wrote *The Very Quiet Cricket*?

     A:   Eric Carle

A 3   Q:   Who is the author of *The Boxcar Children* series?

     A:   Gertrude Chandler Warner

A 4   Q:   Name the author of *Fox in Socks*.

     A:   Dr. Seuss

A 5   Q:   Who is the author of *Hatchet*?

     A:   Gary Paulsen

A 6   Q:   Who writes *The Babysitter's Club* books?

     A:   Ann M. Martin

R 1   Q:   Name a book written by Mark Twain.

     A:   *Huckleberry Finn* or *Tom Sawyer* (answers may vary)

R 2   Q:   Name a book written by Beverly Cleary.

     A:   Ramona series (answers may vary)

R 3   Q:   Daily Double! Name any poem title.

     A:   Answers will vary!

R 4    Q:   What is a popular series about girls of long ago?

      A:   The *American Girl* collection

R 5    Q:   Name a publisher of comic books.

      A:   Marvel (answers may vary)

R 6    Q:   Name a good sports magazine.

      A:   *Beckett, Sports Illustrated, Sports Illustrated for Kids, Inside Stuff* (answers may vary)

CC 1    Q:   Name three types of catalog cards.

      A:   Author, title, and subject

CC 2    Q:   What is in the upper left-hand corner of a catalog card?

      A:   Call number

CC 3    Q:   How does an author's name appear on a catalog card?

      A:   Last name, first name

CC 4    Q:   What word is found in all caps on a catalog card?

      A:   Subject

CC 5    Q:   How many cards are in the catalog card for each book?

      A:   Three (author, title, and subject) or more

CC 6    Q:   If "R" appears on the call number, what does it stand for?

      A:   Reference

D 1    Q:   What does 700–799 stand for?

      A:   Sports, jokes, riddles (accept any suitable answer)

D 2    Q:   What do the 500s stand for?

      A:   Sciences

**(Lifesaver Tool 15.1 continues on page 48.)**

D 3    Q:  Under what number would you find history books?

A:  900s

D 4    Q:  What books are labeled with a 92?

A:  Biographies

D 5    Q:  What does "F" or "Fic" mean in a call number?

A:  Fiction

D 6    Q:  What does it mean when a book's call number begins with a number?

A:  The book is nonfiction

P 1    Q:  What is the term for a book that is not returned on time?

A:  Overdue

P 2    Q:  What is another name for a magazine?

A:  Periodical

P 3    Q:  What is a book that gives synonyms of words?

A:  Thesaurus (dictionary does also)

P 4    Q:  Where is a good place to look to find a map?

A:  Atlas

P 5    Q:  Name a book award for outstanding illustrations.

A:  Caldecott

P 6    Q:  What was Dewey's first name?

A:  Melvil

**Lifesaver Tool 15.1.   Library Jeopardy Questions**

# LIBRARY SKILLS ARE ELEMENTARY!

No matter how hard I try, it always seems as though the end of the year rolls around and I'm not confident I've covered the most important library skills. Sure, I've planned and implemented great lessons, but do the students really have the most important library skills mastered? With these thoughts in mind, I've decided not to work harder (we all work plenty hard, thank you very much!) but to be more intentional in my library lessons. By keeping a checklist handy of the 10 most important skills when planning, I have become more intentional about incorporating those skills into my lessons. I have also retaught skills to students who have not mastered the Top Ten. (Lifesaver Tool 16.1. The Top Ten Elementary Skills) By pairing students who have mastered the skills with students who have not, both students learn a lot! Sure, I teach other important skills throughout the year, but now no year goes by without each student receiving a Top Ten certificate.

## Lifesaver Tips

- As mentioned above, this is just the basic 10 list. It certainly does not include all the skills I teach throughout the school year.

- Read through the list and revise it if there are other skills you feel should make the Top Ten list.

- Get feedback from teachers about the most important skills they would like their class to learn.

 Purchase a book bag for each kindergarten student. Pine Tree Media bags come in a variety of designs and are double-walled. Students put their library books in the bag and the book bag inside their backpack. This procedure has saved many books from mashed bananas and leaking juice boxes.

Randi Hermans, Teacher-Librarian,
East Chilliwack Elementary, Chilliwack, BC

# LIBRARY SKILLS ARE ELEMENTARY!

## TOP TEN SKILLS—GRADES K–1

_____ Students can identify the location of the library.

_____ Students recognize media specialist/aides by name.

_____ Students associate library with books and learning.

_____ Students enjoy storytelling and read-alouds.

_____ Students locate "Easy" books in media center.

_____ Students recognize and name basic parts of a book.

_____ Students associate ABC order with library shelves.

_____ Students can choose their own books.

_____ Students can check out their own books.

_____ Students know that some books are "made up" and that some are "true."

## TOP TEN SKILLS—GRADES 2–3

_____ Students recognize call numbers on "Easy" books.

_____ Students can locate "Easy" books on shelves.

_____ Students begin using "Easy" dictionary for words.

_____ Students demonstrate caring for books.

_____ Students recognize and enjoy Caldecott books.

**(Lifesaver Tool 16.1 continues on page 52.)**

TOP TEN SKILLS—GRADES 2–3 (*continued*)

\_\_\_\_\_ Students distinguish between fiction and nonfiction.

\_\_\_\_\_ Students begin to use "Easy" encyclopedias.

\_\_\_\_\_ Students begin to locate nonfiction books.*

\_\_\_\_\_ Students begin to understand Dewey arrangement.*

\_\_\_\_\_ Students begin to read independently.*

TOP TEN SKILLS—GRADES 4–5

\_\_\_\_\_ Students begin to understand shelving system.

\_\_\_\_\_ Students begin shelving books with shelf markers.

\_\_\_\_\_ Students recognize and name all parts of book.

\_\_\_\_\_ Students begin using maps and globes.

\_\_\_\_\_ Students use dictionaries and encyclopedias.

\_\_\_\_\_ Students begin using other reference tools.

\_\_\_\_\_ Students can locate all types of books.

\_\_\_\_\_ Students read independently for pleasure.

\_\_\_\_\_ Students read independently for information.

\_\_\_\_\_ Students perform research with guided practice.

\_\_\_\_\_ Students can form opinions about what they read.

\_\_\_\_\_ Students can booktalk chosen books.

*Note:* *denotes third-grade skills only.

**Lifesaver Tool 16.1.   The Top Ten Elementary Skills**

# IN THE MIDDLE OF LIBRARY SKILLS

Sometimes just getting the attention of middle school students is a skill in itself. When you do finally get their attention, however, here's a list of basic skills to move them from middle to high—both in school and skills. (Lifesaver Tool 17.1. The Top Ten Middle School Skills)

 Our librarian is experimenting with a flexible schedule. This format allows library lessons to be taught in conjunction with classroom skills. As a result, students see connections between the media center and the subject. The library and lessons have become more meaningful.

Sue Maddux, Fifth-Grade Teacher, Rockville Elementary School, Rockville, IN

# TOP TEN SKILLS—GRADES 6–8

_____ Students can recognize and use all types of reference books.

_____ Students can begin using the *Readers' Guide* with practice.

_____ Students can read and appreciate Newbery Honor books.

_____ Students can outline as a form of research.

_____ Students can take notes while researching.

_____ Students can compile a basic bibliography (eighth grade).

_____ Students can begin to put together a two- to three-page research paper.

_____ Students can compare and contrast books by the same author.

_____ Students can appreciate different genres of literature.

_____ Students can perform independently in the library setting.

**Lifesaver Tool 17.1.   The Top Ten Middle School Skills**

# LIBRARY SKILLS ON HIGH!

Your mood will be high when your students have mastered the skills they need for college—and for life! (Lifesaver Tool 18.1. The Top Ten High School Skills)

## Lifesaver Tips

- To help high school students understand the importance of these skills, you may wish to get a practice SAT test.

- Again, talk with teachers about the most important skills they feel their students should be able to master.

- Use the Internet to research skills, which studies show high school students are not learning.

 Want to be *inspired*? Indiana has a new online database, INSPIRE (http://www. inspire-indiana.net), which includes a magazine article source, online dictionary, newspaper archive, and much more. Indiana residents have free unrestricted access to this site, although residents in other states can gain access to it.

Pamela Bacon

# TOP TEN SKILLS—GRADES 9–12

_____ Students demonstrate research skills.

_____ Students identify reading likes and dislikes.

_____ Students search independently for research and pleasure books.

_____ Students can form a 10-source bibliography.

_____ Students paraphrase research material effectively.

_____ Students understand purpose and format of footnotes.

_____ Students budget research time efficiently.

_____ Students engage in meaningful book discussions.

_____ Students show respect for library's purpose.

_____ Students appreciate literature in many formats.

**Lifesaver Tool 18.1.   The Top Ten High School Skills**

# TEAM UP WITH TEACHERS

Teaming up with teachers can be really easy or downright impossible. It's easy to drag those teachers with whom you are closest into the library with their classes and teach a great thematic unit. Then there are those "other" teachers—the ones who believe your biggest job is to read the paper and drink coffee. It *is* possible, though, to gain support from those teachers if they see that you really can be a support system for them in the classroom. By pulling thematic resources for them, or running off a copy of a professional article on their favorite subject, you can win those teachers to your side—and into the library. (Lifesaver Tool 19.1. Thematic Planning Form)

## Lifesaver Tips

- It's important to walk a fine line with teachers' services. Remember, you're not their servant—you're their partner!

- Go through these forms occasionally to see which teachers you still need to work on—or should I say *with*!

 TEAM = Together Everyone Achieves More. Use this theme and purchase posters, T-shirts, and bookmarks from Argus Company (1-800-860-6762).

Pamela Bacon

# THEMATIC PLANNING FORM

Teacher: _____     Grade: _____

Subject: _____     Class Size: _____

Estimated Time: _____     Date: _____

Title of Lesson: _____

Materials Needed—Teacher:

Materials Needed—Media Specialist:

Procedures:

Evaluation of Students' Learning—Test, Project, or Quiz (below):

Other:

T = Teacher's Responsibility     L = Librarian's Responsibility

**Lifesaver Tool 19.1.   Thematic Planning Form**

From *100 Library Lifesavers.* © 1999 Libraries Unlimited. (800) 237-6124.

# LIBRARY LOTTERY

We've all dreamed of winning the lottery—now here's a way for your students to have a chance, too! No, they don't win real money, but they do win Book Bucks. The Library Lottery (Lifesaver Tool 20.2), in conjunction with the Book Log Form (Lifesaver Tool 20.1) and the Library Lottery Ticket (Lifesaver Tool 20.3), is a motivational reading program for students; it teaches students that reading can be worth millions!

## Lifesaver Tips

- Recommended for grades 6–8.

- Students can play the lottery only if they have turned in a completed Book Log.

- This activity works best on a weekly basis, but can be done quarterly, monthly, or as often as time permits.

- Set a limit that you won't exceed before starting over—100 Book Bucks works well. This limit helps to ensure that no student has too many Book Bucks at a time.

- To involve the administration, ask your principal to roll the dice for you.

- The winners can be announced over the intercom with the regular announcements.

- Because this is a modified form of gambling, be sure to obtain permission and support from your administration before using the Library Lottery.

 Read aloud *The Lottery* by Shirley Jackson to young adult classes.

Pamela Bacon

## Procedures

1. Each time a student turns in a completed Book Log, give him or her a Library Lottery Ticket.

2. The student fills out the Library Lottery Ticket with five numbers (in order).

3. Roll the dice to see if any students picked the correct numbers.

4. If no student held a winning ticket, the kitty is increased.

5. If the lottery reaches $100 and no student has chosen the correct numbers, start over with 25 Book Bucks!

6. Keep Book Logs in the game until someone wins.

7. After a winner is chosen, discard all Book Logs and start over!

8. This activity can easily be adapted for high school use when a different prize is chosen (extra credit points, perhaps?!?).

# BOOK LOG

Name: _____          Teacher: _____

| DATE | TITLE | AUTHOR | PAGES READ |
|------|-------|--------|------------|
|      |       |        |            |
|      |       |        |            |
|      |       |        |            |
|      |       |        |            |
|      |       |        |            |
|      |       |        |            |
|      |       |        |            |
|      |       |        |            |
|      |       |        |            |
|      |       |        |            |
|      |       |        |            |
|      |       |        |            |
|      |       |        |            |
|      |       |        |            |
|      |       |        |            |
|      |       |        |            |
|      |       |        |            |
|      |       |        |            |

LOTTERY TICKET RECD._____ LIBRARIAN'S SIGNATURE _____

**Lifesaver Tool 20.1.** **Book Log Form**

# LIBRARY LOTTERY: THE SIX Ws OF WINNING!

## What is Library Lottery?

A motivational reading program for grades 6–8.

## What must I do?

- Turn in a completed Book Log.
- Pick up your Library Lottery Ticket from the media center.
- Fill out your ticket.
- Place your ticket into the lottery basket.
- Wait to see if you're a winner!

## Who can play?

You can—if you read and turn in a Book Log!

## Where can I play Library Lottery?

In the library—where else?!?

## When are lottery numbers chosen?

Every _____!

## Why should I play Library Lottery?

Because it's a great way to have fun reading and win prizes at the same time! If you're lucky, that is!

**Lifesaver Tool 20.2.   The Six Ws of Winning**

From *100 Library Lifesavers.* © 1999 Libraries Unlimited. (800) 237-6124.

# $$$ LIBRARY LOTTERY $$$

Name_____ Grade_____

Teacher_____ Date _____

Pick any five numbers between 1 and 6.

You can use a number more than once.

To win, all numbers must be in the correct order!

_____   _____   _____   _____   _____

Good luck—keep reading to win!

# $$$ LIBRARY LOTTERY $$$

Name_____ Grade_____

Teacher_____ Date _____

Pick any five numbers between 1 and 6.

You can use a number more than once.

To win, all numbers must be in the correct order!

_____   _____   _____   _____   _____

Good luck—keep reading to win!

**Lifesaver Tool 20.3.   Library Lottery Ticket**

# WHAT A CRITIC!

A step above the typical book report, this form encourages students to write a Siskel-and-Ebert-type review. The focus is on letting other readers know whether they should (or should not!) read the reviewed book. (Lifesaver Tool 21.1. Book Review Form)

## Lifesaver Tips

- Pay students five Book Bucks for each review.

- Keep fiction reviews in one binder and nonfiction reviews in another for organizational purposes.

- By filing the reviews under the author's last name, students can easily check a review before checking out.

- Remember, even negative reviews are a chance for students to express their opinions.

- For every negative review, try to get a positive review. This way, students see that reading likes (and dislikes!) are personal choices.

- Well-written reviews make excellent additions to a school newspaper or library newsletter.

- During open house, laminate and post reviews next to the book.

- For extra Book Bucks, ask students to add illustrations to the book review.

IIII➡ Looking for a quick-and-easy bulletin board idea? Purchase a Nike poster with a big "swoosh" (the Nike symbol). Post the poster on a bulletin board with the slogan *Just Do It—Return Books on Time!* For Nike product information, call 1-800-352-NIKE.

Pamela Bacon

# BOOK REVIEW

Author's last name_____

Written by _____ Teacher_____

Title of book_____

Author_____

Copyright date_____ Rating _____

COVER STORY!

Even though you can't always judge a book by its cover, did this book's cover grab your attention? _____

How could the cover have been improved?

_____

_____

INSIDE EDITION!

Describe the most exciting part of the book (conflict), but be sure not to give away the ending!!!

_____

_____

_____

Would you recommend this book to other readers? Why or why not?

_____

_____

Does our media center have other books by this author? If so, list two other titles below:

    1. _____

    2. _____

**Lifesaver Tool 21.1.   Book Review Form**

# BOOK SHOP & SWAP!

Every year, I am amazed by the incredible number of students who participate in this event. I knew it was a great idea and I'm thrilled students think so, too!

## Lifesaver Tips

- Set a time limit for books to be brought in. For the sake of manageability, I recommend not allowing books to be brought in on the day of the swap.

- Include procedures in letter to parents. (Lifesaver Tool 22.1. Book Swap Procedures)

- Give a Book Swap Ticket for each book brought in. (Lifesaver Tool 22.2. Book Swap Ticket Samples)

- Stress to students that all books should be handled gently. Even great books usually aren't chosen if they have damaged or torn covers.

- Allow teachers to draw names to determine the order of classes for the swap. You can use regular library time, but you almost always hear complaints from the classes that have to choose last!

- Label tables with categories. Fiction, nonfiction, sports, and mysteries are just some of the categories that make book selection run a little smoother.

- For an elementary school, put books on tables according to reading levels. Otherwise, it never fails that a kindergarten student loves an exciting cover on a chapter book!

- This activity also works great at the high school level. I strongly recommend, however, previewing books for acceptability before the swap!

- Allowing students to purchase additional books with Book Bucks is fun. However, make sure this is done only after all students have had a chance to cash their Book Swap Tickets.

Tired of the traditional book swap? Then hold a cyber swap! Students e-mail other students and then use snail mail to make the trade!

Nancy Witty, Media Specialist,
Rockville Elementary School, Rockville, IN

# BOOK SWAP PROCEDURES

Date: _____

Dear Parents:

This is an opportunity for students to trade books they have already enjoyed for a different "new" book.

Let me explain . . .

1.  Students in grades _____ may bring a *maximum* of three (3) books to school if he or she wishes to participate in the book swap. *This is not a required activity!*

2.  Classroom or homeroom teachers will collect books and give students a Book Swap Ticket for each book received. Teachers will not accept books that are tattered or books that are not suitable.

3.  Books will be collected until _____.

4.  The Book Swap will be held in the media center on:

    _____(date and time). Students will be able to redeem their tickets for books on that day.

A quick reminder that students should be certain of their choices before bringing them to school. Once a book(s) is brought in, the swap is permanent and the book(s) cannot be returned.

Thank you for your support of this activity. If you have questions concerning the Book Swap, please contact me at _____.

Sincerely,

_____
Media Specialist

**Lifesaver Tool 22.1.** **Book Swap Procedures**

# BOOK SWAP TICKET

From *100 Library Lifesavers.* © 1999 Libraries Unlimited. (800) 237-6124.

**Lifesaver Tool 22.2.   Book Swap Ticket Samples**

# TESTING, TESTING, ONE, TWO, THREE!

Have you taught the card catalog for years, but still aren't sure if your sixth-graders have mastered the basic Dewey skills? Well, give this quick-and-easy pretest and find out. You'll have their number in no time! (Lifesaver Tool 23.1. Library Pretest Form)

## Lifesaver Tips

- To save time, have students exchange and grade tests.

- Instead of recording scores, simply write down pass/fail marks.

- For students who pass, offer exciting enrichment choices.

- Showing a tasteful movie of a classic book is always a popular enrichment choice!

- Reteach basics to students who didn't "dew" well.

- Give the same test again after reviewing. Scores should go way up!

- Book Bucks make nice prizes for students who pass the test—either the first or second time.

Answers to the pretest are as follows:

1) T; 2) T; 3) F; 4) T; 5) T; 6) T; 7) F; 8) F; 9) F; and 10) T

 After you're automated, use card catalogs to store cassettes, office supplies, and other items! After all, the catalog is almost an antique!

Pamela Bacon

# LIBRARY PRETEST

Name_____

Grade_____

T    F    1.    There are three main ways to find a book using the card catalog.

T    F    2.    One way to locate a book in the card catalog is by title.

T    F    3.    Another way to locate a book in the card catalog is by call number.

T    F    4.    To find the book *The Red Corvette* by SUBJECT, you could look under "R" for Red.

T    F    5.    To find a book by R. L. Stine by AUTHOR, you could look under "S" for Stine.

T    F    6.    When looking up a book by the TITLE, you should ignore the words *a*, *an*, and *the*.

T    F    7.    The first step to finding a certain book is to look on a shelf.

T    F    8.    To find a book called *The Grapes of Wrath*, look under "T," the first word of the title.

T    F    9.    If you do not know the title of a book, you probably won't be able to find it.

T    F    10.    The call number tells you where to find the book in the library.

**Lifesaver Tool 23.1.**   **Library Pretest**

# MISSING MAGAZINE METHOD

Are missing magazines in the media center making you mad? (Talk about alliteration!) If they are, try this method! Because the idea is so simple, I really hesitated about putting it in this book. The more I thought about it, though, I realized this magazine inventory was just one more tool that makes my job a little easier. I hope it makes yours easier, too. (Lifesaver Tool 24.1. Missing Magazines Form)

## Lifesaver Tips

- Because this procedure is so simple, it's a great chore to keep student helpers busy and on task.

- Student helpers can work independently on this task!

- Although there is really nothing to be done when a magazine is missing, it's important to know whether it's available when students are using *The Readers' Guide*.

- When a magazine is missing, make a note on the front of the magazine holder.

- This procedure also helps keep magazines neat and in order.

- Discarded magazines are nice additions to the Book Swap (see Library Lifesaver 22).

- This lifesaver is an excellent place to record discarded periodicals.

- Include the number of years magazines are kept in your library policy manual.

 Because periodicals are so expensive, be sure to get teacher and student input before renewing. Also, if you get a magazine or newspaper online, don't buy the print version, too.

Pamela Bacon

# MISSING MAGAZINES

Title of Magazine_____

Year_____

January      _____

February     _____

March        _____

April        _____

May          _____

June         _____

July         _____

August       _____

September    _____

October      _____

November     _____

December     _____

Comments:

_____

_____

_____

_____

**Lifesaver Tool 24.1.   Missing Magazines Form**

# TAKE TIME FOR A GOOD 'BOO'K!

Halloween is a great time to begin this motivational reading activity. (Lifesaver Tool 25.1. Monthly Reading Contest) Fall has set in, students are more adjusted, and now they're ready to read! Although I originally designed the idea for students, I found elementary teachers really like to participate, too!

## Lifesaver Tips

- As stated above, use the activity with students, teachers, or both!

- Each time a student (or teacher!) reads a ghost, Halloween, or otherwise scary story, that person fills out a ghost with his or her name and the title of the book read.

- Each week, draw out a name(s) for a prize.

- Students' prizes can be Book Bucks or any other incentive that might entice them to read. (Isn't it sad that a great book doesn't always do it?)

- A "free" 15-minute break is a nice prize when a participating teacher's name is drawn. It's also a perfect way to lure a class into the media center for a great scary read-aloud!

- Attach a big ghost holding a trick-or-treat bag to the library door for an easy way to decorate and to draw students' attention to the contest at the same time.

- Completed ghosts can be placed right in the bag.

- This activity can easily be adapted for any month of the school year. The list of monthly ideas is a nice list to keep in your files for a rainy day.

 *Wolf Rider: A Tale of Terror* by Avi is a great read-aloud for middle grades. It's so good, it's scary!

Pamela Bacon

# MONTHLY READING CONTEST

## THEME IDEAS

August/September Theme:              Fall into a Good Book!
Entry Form: Leaves

October Theme:                       Take Time for a Good "Boo"k!
Entry Form: Ghost

November Theme:                      Don't Be a Turkey—Read!
Entry Form: Turkey

December Theme:                      Books Are "Deer" Friends!
Entry Form: Reindeer

January Theme:                       Warm Up with a Good Book!
Entry Form: Mitten

February Theme:                      Love a Book!
Entry Form: Heart

March Theme:                         March in for a Good Book!
Entry Form: Flower

April Theme:                         Hop in for a Great Book!
Entry Form: Bunny

May Theme:                           Race in for a Great Book!
Entry Form: Race Car

From *100 Library Lifesavers.* © 1999 Libraries Unlimited. (800) 237-6124.

**Lifesaver Tool 25.1.   Monthly Reading Contest**

# PROGRAM KIDS TO READ!

Whether we like it or not, television is an important part of our students' lives. Sure, we'd rather they read more and watch television less, but if they're going to tune in, we might as well make it work for us before they tune out! (Lifesaver Tool 26.1. Channel Your Thoughts and Read Form)

## Lifesaver Tips

- Purchase DEMCO posters of television celebrities encouraging students to read (1-800-356-1200).

- Purchase and/or spotlight biographies of teenage stars. (Yes, they change rapidly, but while they're hot, the books will be in great demand!)

- Purchase *Books—The Other Channel* posters from DEMCO (1-800-356-1200).

- Start a Channel Your Thoughts and Read week. The idea is that students don't watch television for an entire week!

- Use a library class period to write to celebrities; use popular reference books to find addresses. The *World Almanac and Book of*

*Facts* could be used to write to the stars via the television network stations.

- Cut out and display pictures of stars promoting books. These ads are becoming popular in magazines and newspapers around the country.

- Obviously, this lifesaver, if adapted, could easily be used with both junior and senior high school students.

 If you do decide to turn on the television, make sure it's worth watching. Grace Products (1-800-527-4014) produces some of the best videos I've seen. The "going back in time" format is a definite kid pleaser and the high quality is a librarian pleaser.

Pamela Bacon

# CHANNEL YOUR THOUGHTS
# AND READ!

To celebrate National Library Week, which is planned for the week of
_____, students are asked to turn off their
favorite television shows and channel their thoughts to books instead.
Each night that he or she turns off the television and reads, complete the
attached form. Students can then bring their completed forms to the media
center. A daily drawing for free books will be held! Happy reading!

P.S. Parents might try this activity, too!

_____ channeled his or her thoughts and read
       (Student's Name)

_____
             (Book Title)

by _____.
      (Author)

Date: _____

Parent's/Guardian's Signature _____.

**Lifesaver Tool 26.1.   Channel Your Thoughts and Read! Form**

# DUST OFF YOUR ELECTRONIC BOOKSHELF!

For those of you who still rely on the tried-and-true Electronic Bookshelf reading program, these lifesavers will come in handy!

## Lifesaver Tips

- Laminate and post Lifesaver Tool 27.1 (30 Steps to Success Handout) by your computer station.

- Copy, laminate, and distribute the same tool to teachers who use this program—it's sure to prevent a lot of the same questions teachers and media specialists are asked over and over again.

- Even though the directions are posted, students would rather ask than find out the information for themselves. Make them read and follow the steps so that they'll find success—on their own!

- Use the Electronic Bookshelf Reading Program Form (Lifesaver Tool 27.2) to keep track of students' progress. Because scores are available from the computer, this step isn't necessary, but might be useful in certain situations.

- Give Book Bucks to students who correctly answer all quiz questions!

- Run off Electronic Bookshelf Scores (EBS) for teachers at the end of each grading period. Teachers really appreciate this service and many give students extra credit points based on their scores.

- During the summer, make up your own quizzes on popular new books. Or, even better, ask students to make them after they read the book!

 If you don't have the EBS program, choose a set of 20 award-winning favorite books. Assign a class the task of reading the book and then of writing a 10-question multiple choice quiz. Ask library helpers to type the quizzes and you'll have your own old-fashioned version of the Electronic Bookshelf program (with manual scoring)!

Pamela Bacon

# 30 STEPS TO SUCCESS!

How to Take an Electronic Bookshelf Quiz:

1. Put Electronic Bookshelf program disk in drive 1 (left).
2. Put disk with teacher's name in drive 2 (right).
3. Turn on computer.
4. Tell computer you are using two (2) drives.
5. Press return.
6. Tell computer "No" when it asks if you need directions.
7. Take out the program disk in drive 1 (left).
8. Put in disk that has a book quiz on it (yellow label).
9. Press return.
10. Type correct number of the quiz you want to take.
11. Press return.
12. Type in your first name.
13. Press return.
14. Type in your middle initial.
15. Press return.
16. Type in your last name.
17. Press return.
18. Type in your teacher's last name (group name).
19. Press return.
20. Type "Y" for yes.
21. Type "Y" if you have taken a quiz this year.
22. Type "N" if you have not taken a quiz this year.
23. Always type in your name exactly the same way (e.g., Jonathan instead of Jon).
24. Answer each question.
25. Press return after each answer.
26. Read your grade for the quiz.
27. Press return.
28. Type "N" if you don't want to review your answers.
29. Type "Y" if you would like to review your answers.
30. Type "N" if you do not want to take another quiz.

**Lifesaver Tool 27.1.   30 Steps to Success Handout**

# ELECTRONIC BOOKSHELF
# READING PROGRAM

**Step 1**

I read the following book:

_____

_____

_____

_____

_____

_____

_____

_____

_____

**Step 2**

Computer quiz

Score: _____

**Step 3**

Book Bucks earned:

_____

Student's Signature_____

Teacher's/Parent's Signature _____

**Lifesaver Tool 27.2.   Electronic Bookshelf Reading Program Form**

# ON YOUR HONOR!

No matter how many notices we send or how many reminders we give, sometimes overdues abound! Although teachers basically understand and support the library policy about not allowing a student with overdues to check out books, there is sometimes still a problem when teachers hold silent reading in their classrooms. The students with overdues undoubtedly have nothing to read—of course, the overdue book is somewhere at home! Because of these concerns, I decided to try the Honor System and see how it worked. The "truth" is, the system worked great!

## Lifesaver Tips

- Be sure that all Honor System books are clearly marked with a label. (Lifesaver Tool 28.1. Sample Honor System Book Labels)

- Cut out the label and tape securely on the front and back of the book with clear packing tape.

- Students who have overdues may check out only an Honor System book.

- Honor books are not checked out—instead, they are just borrowed and returned. When books are gone, they're gone. (I had doubts about loaning Honor System books to students with overdues, but the Honor System books are almost always returned right away. The students seem to like this responsibility!)

- Obviously, if students abuse this privilege, they may no longer use the Honor System.

- This Honor System also works well for avid readers who like to check out more than the maximum number of weekly books.

- The Honor System Book Procedures Handout (Lifesaver Tool 28.2) is a sign that you can put up beside the Honor System books to explain how the system works.

 Speaking of honor, honor sixth-grade students at the end of the year by setting off helium balloons. Inside the balloon, place the student's name, a favorite book title, and a request for finders to respond with *their* favorite book titles.

Pamela Bacon

# HONOR SYSTEM BOOK LABEL

**HONOR
SYSTEM
BOOK**

**HONOR
SYSTEM
BOOK**

**HONOR
SYSTEM
BOOK**

**HONOR
SYSTEM
BOOK**

**HONOR
SYSTEM
BOOK**

**HONOR
SYSTEM
BOOK**

**HONOR
SYSTEM
BOOK**

**HONOR
SYSTEM
BOOK**

**HONOR
SYSTEM
BOOK**

**HONOR
SYSTEM
BOOK**

<u>**Lifesaver Tool 28.1.**</u>   **Sample Honor System Book Labels**

# HONOR SYSTEM BOOK PROCEDURES

You may borrow an Honor System book if

1.  You forgot your books at home or

2.  You would like to check out extra books.

Return these books as soon as you are finished!

If you would like to donate quality paperbacks for our Honor System, please check with your library media specialist!

Thank you!

From *100 Library Lifesavers.* © 1999 Libraries Unlimited. (800) 237-6124.

**Lifesaver Tool 28.2.**   **Honor System Book Procedures Handout**

# NEED A LITTLE CLASS?

Now that life licenses are a thing of the past and two classes are required to renew teaching licenses, are you (or your teachers) constantly looking for courses to take? With the increasing popularity and abundance of distance education courses, classes can now be taken from the comfort of your own home or from wherever you want to be!

## Lifesaver Tips

- Be sure to check the course fees before enrolling; some are much higher than others.

- Some schools allow you to take individual classes, but others want you to enroll in an entire program. Be sure to check your bulletin for complete registration information.

- Make sure the school is highly accredited before enrolling. You don't want to take a course and find that it can't be transferred to a traditional college.

- Talk to faculty members before enrolling to see whether the course is right for you. Most staff members will be honest about their expectations.

- Ask for names of former students and call them for references.

- Keep up with the coursework—most independent study courses have a deadline of one year.

- Keep Lifesaver Tool 29.1 (List of Schools Offering Graduate Correspondence and/or Distance Education Courses) in a handy file for you and let teachers know you have it!

 Send a nice note to a teacher you know is working hard on a class—they'll appreciate the kind gesture.

Pamela Bacon

# SCHOOLS OFFERING GRADUATE CORRESPONDENCE AND/OR DISTANCE EDUCATION COURSES

1. Lee Canter & Associates
   1-800-669-9011
   Earn three semester hours of graduate credit via video.

2. Graduate School, USDA
   1-202-690-4280   http://grad.usda.gov/corres/corpro.html/
   Take courses and/or earn certification in a number of graduate-level courses.

3. University of Alaska Distance Education Program
   1-907-786-4400   http://www.dist-ed.uaf.edu/ualc/course.html
   Earn a degree or take courses at the undergraduate or graduate level. Correspondence and online courses are available.

4. California State University—Dominguez Hills
   1-310-243-3743   http://www.csudh.edu/

5. UCLA Extension Online Courses
   1-800-784-8436   http://www.then.com/ *or*
   http://www.OnlineLearning.net/
   Choose from more than 50 online courses.

6. Bureau of Education & Research
   1-800-735-3503
   Hundreds of one-day workshops are available on a wide variety of educational topics. One graduate credit can be earned for each completed workshop.

7. Penn State University—Distance Education
   1-800-252-3592   http://www.distance-ed-review.com/pgmreview8.html
   PSU offers more than 250 credit and noncredit courses via e-mail, video, and snail mail.

8. Indiana University
   1-800-334-1011   http://www.extend.indiana.edu/
   One of the world's best independent study programs (and I'm not saying that just because I'm from Indiana!). Choose from more than 300 undergraduate and graduate courses from 40 departments. An associate's or bachelor's degree in general studies can be earned entirely through independent study.

**Lifesaver Tool 29.1.**   **List of Schools Offering Graduate Correspondence and/or Distance Education Courses**

# NO MORE MISSING VCRs!

Are you constantly looking for a good sign-up form for audiovisual equipment? Well, your search is now over. I hope your search for borrowed equipment will be, too!

## Lifesaver Tips

- Keep the AV Form (Lifesaver Tool 30.1. Audiovisual Sign-Up Form) handy on a clipboard next to your audiovisual equipment.

- If feasible, keep another AV Form in the office by the staff mailboxes. It's not easy to keep track of two forms, but you might find more people tend to use them that way!

- Post a blank calendar in the same places for reserving audiovisual equipment.

- The forms include both periods and time slots for use in elementary or secondary schools.

- Use brightly colored stickers with numbers to mark your audio-visual equipment. It not only makes sign-ups easier, but it makes inventory quicker, too!

- Keep old sign-up sheets in a file. When it's time to do your annual report, it's easy to see how much your audiovisual equipment circulates. These numbers are also useful in justifying purchasing new equipment.

 Use neon-colored stickers and mark the television, cart, and videocassette recorder with the same number. It's a good way to keep your tracking to a minimum.

Pamela Bacon

# SIGN-UP FORM FOR
# AUDIOVISUAL MATERIALS

WEEK OF _____

| Teacher | # | Equipment | 8-9 P. 1 | 9-10 P. 2 | 10-11 P. 3 | 11-12 P. 4 | 12-1 P. 5 | 1-2 P. 6 | 2-3 P. 7 |
|---|---|---|---|---|---|---|---|---|---|
| | | | | | | | | | |
| | | | | | | | | | |
| | | | | | | | | | |
| | | | | | | | | | |
| | | | | | | | | | |
| | | | | | | | | | |
| | | | | | | | | | |
| | | | | | | | | | |
| | | | | | | | | | |
| | | | | | | | | | |
| | | | | | | | | | |
| | | | | | | | | | |

*Note:*  Please see the media specialist to check for equipment reserves!

From *100 Library Lifesavers.* © 1999 Libraries Unlimited. (800) 237-6124.

**Lifesaver Tool 30.1.  Audiovisual Sign-Up Form**

# YOU ASKED FOR IT!

This simple form is a great time-saver; not only does it give quick feedback, it provides more effective communication to teachers and students. (Lifesaver Tool 31.1. You Asked for It! Form) We know we work hard, but it's nice to let others indirectly know it, too!

 Each time an interlibrary loan book arrives, mark the due date on your calendar. Not only will you remember to return the item, you'll be reminded to send the return notice out, too!

Pamela Bacon

# YOU ASKED FOR IT!

Dear _____ ,

Class _____

You asked for it . . . and we got it!

The book, _____
that you requested is here!

We will save the book until: _____ .

If you no longer want to borrow this item, please let us know!

Thank you,

The Media Center

**Lifesaver Tool 31.1.   You Asked for It! Form**

# BOOK MARKER

The Book Marker is a great way to mark those books cluttering your office shelves. Because there are so many reasons for books to be out of circulation, I came up with a checklist to organize and keep track of those odds-and-ends book jobs. Sure, you can use a sticky note, but this form adds more organization and detail. And, because it's taped on, it won't fall off. On this form, an "X" marks the spot—literally!

## Lifesaver Tips

- If desired, this form could easily be enlarged on a copier. I prefer it small (bookmark size!) so that it fits onto paperbacks and videotapes.

- The Book Marker Form (Lifesaver Tool 32.1) is a great way to let student assistants or library volunteers know what needs to be done with problem books.

- The comment section is great for writing down additional book notes or jobs not on the checklist.

- Because there is a date for when the Book Marker is filled out and a date for when the job is completed, you can see at a glance which jobs have priority.

- If desired, the form could be copied onto different shades of paper. For example, books needing to be processed could be green; books needing repairs could be yellow.

- The form can be placed within the pages of a book; however, I prefer to tape it directly to the front of the book.

 I bookmark my library automation technical assistance phone number and my customer code number on my computer and on a Post-it note by the phone. Now, when I need to call them quickly, I'm never fumbling around for the number or code. Because we're running a new library with a new automation system, I've needed to call the number quite frequently!

Joanne Ladewig,
Information Center Director,
Fairgrove Academy, Valinda, CA

# BOOK MARKER

Date: _____

Author: _____

Title: _____

___ Needs processing.

___ Needs shelflist card.

___ Enter into computer.

___ Needs repair—p. ____

___ Needs spine label.

___ Needs discarding.

___ Other: _____

Comments:

_____

_____

_____

_____

Date completed:

_____

By:

_____

**Lifesaver Tool 32.1.   Book Marker Form**

# MEDIA CENTER MEMO

Because there's always so much we have to do, the Media Center Memo Form (Lifesaver Tool 33.1) is extremely useful. Though somewhat generic, this form is also the most used. Having a stack on hand makes immediate feedback possible in a matter of seconds. Got a minute? That's all you'll need!

 Save yourself time and hassle by saving a copy of absolutely everything you send out!

Pamela Bacon

# MEDIA CENTER MEMO

DATE: _____ DEPARTMENT: _____

TO: _____

_____ 1.   I am currently ordering new materials.
           Please advise if you or your department have specific
           requests.

_____ 2.   The following item is in the media center:

           _____

_____ 3.   Please return the following material to the media center:

           _____

_____ 4.   Feel free to keep the attached material or pass it on.

_____ 5.   The attached material is here on preview. Please review

           and return by _____.

_____ 6.   The media center is reserved for your class on _____

           _____. What materials will you

           be using?_____

_____ 7.   Other: _____

           _____

           _____

           _____

**Lifesaver Tool 33.1.   Media Center Memo Form**

# GOOD BOOKS—THEY'RE IN THE BAG!

This activity is a great way to get students focused at the beginning of library class. All you need for this lesson is a brown lunch bag and a little creativity!

## Lifesaver Tips

- In a brown lunch bag, place objects or symbols that go with a book.

- Pull the items out of the bag one at a time.

- Students try to guess the title of the mystery book.

- The first student to guess correctly can win a prize or check out an extra book!

- This activity can work much like a booktalk if students haven't read the book.

- Once students are used to the idea, they can make up their own bags and try to get students to guess the mystery book.

- Post a sign-up sheet, allowing one student per week to bring a bag!

- The bags can easily be kept from year to year for a fun and quick activity.

- To give you the idea, here are some items for E. B. White's *Charlotte's Web*: a rubber spider, a picture of a pig, a toy farm tractor, etc.

- For another activity using brown lunch bags, make a bag for each classroom. In the bag, place bookmarks, Book Bucks, pencils, or any little surprise during book week. Lifesaver Tool 34.1 (Sample Bag-a-Book Labels) includes the label to put on the bag to make this idea immediately usable!

 I carry a bag of tools: scissors, staple puller, calculator, and laser pointer (and headache remedy!). I find that my desk is open season when I'm not there, and I can't count on having these things handy when I need them!

Pamela Gelbmann, Media Generalist, Madison Elementary School, Blaine, MN

# BAG-A-BOOK LABELS

**Lifesaver Tool 34.1.**   **Sample Bag-a-Book Labels**

# YOU'RE IN GOOD FORM!

With all we've got to do, it's not easy keeping up good communication with teachers. The following two lifesaver tools can help. Before you "form" the opinion that better communication is hopeless, try these lifesavers!

## Lifesaver Tips

- It's easy to use the Just Wanted You to Know Form (Lifesaver Tool 35.1) when the class's behavior is bad. Just try to use it just as much when you catch the class being good!

- Keep stacks of the Help Form (Lifesaver Tool 35.2) handy in the media center, but also run off plenty of forms and distribute to teachers at the beginning of each school year.

- Forms similar to these are available to purchase, but these are much cheaper!

 When a class shows consistent good behavior, we play a library trivia game that I always carry with me. To make it, I cut index cards in half and have questions and answers from popular books on them. This simple activity is a lifesaver when I have a few spare moments at the end of library class!

Pamela Gelbmann, Media Generalist, Madison Elementary School, Blaine, MN

# JUST WANTED YOU TO KNOW!

# HELP!

Class: _____

I need materials on:

Comments: _____

_____

_____

_____

_____

_____

_____

_____

_____

_____

_____

_____

_____

_____

_____

_____

_____

_____

_____

_____

_____

Teacher: _____

_____

Return to Media Center!

From the Media Center

The items you requested will be delivered ASAP!

**Lifesaver Tool 35.1.   Just Wanted You to Know Form**

**Lifesaver Tool 35.2.   Help Form**

# GET ON TRACK!

Keeping up with the routing of professional magazines is never easy, but this tracking form can help. Now, getting your teachers to pass it on is another story . . .

## Lifesaver Tips

- Teacher accountability is added because there is a place for the media specialist to check off on the Magazine Tracking Form (Lifesaver Tool 36.1) when the magazine has been returned.

- I've never been brave enough to try this, but you could always refuse to let the new issue be released until the old one has been returned!

- Many times teachers themselves will help prevent tracking problems.

- From time to time, switch the order of the names for fairness so that no teacher is always the last one to get the magazines full of helpful teaching ideas.

- Give teachers input into the selection of magazines. Take a quick survey each year to see if a magazine should be renewed or another one purchased in its place.

- Remind teachers that the success of tracking depends on their passing the magazine on in a timely manner. If a tracking system doesn't work, the next option is to make the magazines available on a first come, first served basis! That should encourage a quick response!

- The Missing Magazines Form (Lifesaver Tool 24.1) can be used as a checklist to know when issues have been returned by the teacher. A student assistant could easily be assigned to keep track of distributing professional magazines to teachers and checking off the forms when magazines are returned to the library. That way, your time is free for assisting students or performing more difficult tasks.

 For a touch of home, place wicker baskets full of magazines around the classroom for easy access. Baskets with handles also make great totes to carry things home from school—I love Longaberger!

Wendy Auman, Teacher,
Walnut Elementary School, New Ross, IN

# MAGAZINE TRACKING FORM

Title of Magazine: _____

Month: _____

      Teachers: Please check off your name after you've finished and pass the magazine on to the next person as soon as possible. Thanks!

_____ Teacher: _____

_____ Teacher: _____

_____ Teacher: _____

_____ Teacher: _____

_____ Teacher: _____

_____ Teacher: _____

_____ Teacher: _____

_____ Media Specialist—Returned

Comments: _____

_____

_____

_____

_____

_____

_____

**Lifesaver Tool 36.1.** **Magazine Tracking Form**

# BOOK
# A PREVIEW!

After years of constant telephone interruptions from salespeople, I finally decided that if you can't beat 'em (and sometimes we'd like to!), join 'em! Before I join, however, I ask a lot of questions and make sure the preview will be to my benefit. You certainly don't want this to end up being a sneak preview! (Lifesaver Tool 37.1. Book Preview Form)

## Lifesaver Tips

- How long can I keep the books?

- Who pays the return shipping and handling charges?

- Can you arrange for the books to be picked up directly from the media center?

- Can I choose to keep just some of the books or must I keep them all?

- Do I receive a substantial discount?

- If the books are kept longer than the specified time, what is the penalty?

- Does the time start from when I receive the books or before?

- Are there any sample books to keep?

 Before agreeing to preview, always get the name and telephone number of the sales representative.

Pamela Bacon

# BOOK PREVIEW FORM

Date Received: _____ Company: _____

Date for Books to Be Returned:_____

Comments: _____

_____

_____

_____

Titles Purchased Now:

1. _____

2. _____

3. _____

4. _____

5. _____

Titles to Purchase Later:

1. _____

2. _____

3. _____

4. _____

5. _____

**Lifesaver Tool 37.1.   Book Preview Form**

*From 100 Library Lifesavers.* © 1999 Libraries Unlimited. (800) 237-6124.

# WORKING ON STUDENT HELPERS

Student helpers are certainly a "novel" bunch! On one hand, I've had student assistants who could have run the library without me. On the other hand, I've had student assistants I've had to run after. You know the type—they're always taking advantage of their student-helper status to roam the halls! If you've ever felt that it would be easier to do the job yourself rather than try to explain it to a student, then hopefully these lifesavers—and your student helpers—will work! (Lifesaver Tool 38.1. Student Assistant Application Form)

## Lifesaver Tips

- Intended use: junior high/middle school. See Lifesaver 64 for high school helpers.

- Don't hire student assistants too early in the school year. When you don't know a student well, you may not make a good decision.

- Sometimes it's better to have no helpers at all. If you don't feel any qualified students have volunteered, don't "hire" any until next semester.

- If at all possible, try not to have best friends as student helpers. They often get along a little too well, and don't get a whole lot done.

- Don't overlook the at-risk students. I've had difficult students turn around when given a chance!

- Try to give as much structure as possible to student helpers. A weekly job list works well to keep both of you focused.

 Rather than have a permanent student assistant, I use volunteers from study hall on an as-needed basis. I find the student who wants to get out of study hall usually works harder than the student assistant who is assigned to me each day.

Pamela Bacon

# STUDENT ASSISTANT APPLICATION

Name: _____

Grade: _____      Age:_____

What periods or times are you available to work? (lunch, study halls, before school, after school)

_____

Do you have previous library experience? _____

If yes, please describe: _____

_____

Why do you think you would make a good student assistant?_____

_____

_____

What are your hobbies? _____

What is your best subject? _____

What is your worst subject?_____

What types of grades do you normally earn?_____

Have you ever worked outside of school? _____ If so, where? _____

List three references (coaches, teachers, employers, or others who will speak highly of you):

    1. _____

    2. _____

    3. _____

**Lifesaver Tool 38.1.   Student Assistant Application Form**

# READING IS OUT OF THIS WORLD!

Don't just tell students that reading is out of this world—show them with this lifesaver!

## Lifesaver Tips

- Each time you, or a teacher, read aloud a book focusing on another country, place a colored push pin on the map at that location.

- Encourage students to read books focusing on a variety of different countries. As students fill out the following tickets, more push pins fill the map! (Lifesaver Tool 39.1. Reading Is out of This World Ticket)

- Put reading tickets in a jar in the media center.

- At the end of a designated time, pull out names of students who earn free books.

- Holding this activity just before a book fair is a nice way to reward students with free book fair books.

- Fairy tales from other countries are perfect for this activity.

- This activity can work for almost all grade levels. At the high school level, the tickets could be exchanged for a short book report. You could easily team with the world history teacher on a variation of this activity.

 Want to collaborate? Check out Roger Taylor's site (http://www.rogertaylor.com/) full of integrated thematic units and curriculum tie-ins. For a small fee, you'll find priceless information.

Tamora K. Brewer, Assistant Principal,
Tzouanakis Intermediate School,
Greencastle, IN

# READING IS OUT OF THIS WORLD!

NAME: _____

Grade: _____ Teacher/Homeroom: _____

Country: _____

Title of book: _____

_____

NAME: _____

Grade: _____ Teacher/Homeroom: _____

Country: _____

Title of book: _____

_____

NAME: _____

Grade: _____ Teacher/Homeroom: _____

Country: _____

Title of book: _____

_____

**Lifesaver Tool 39.1.   Reading Is out of This World Ticket**

# DEWEY, WE'VE GOT YOUR NUMBER!

After teaching the Dewey Decimal System for years, I've finally found a way to help students remember those numbers and what they stand for. (Lifesaver Tool 40.1. The Dewey Song) You'll be singing a tune when your students finally know their Dewey numbers!

## Lifesaver Tips

- I suggest teaching only one section a week.

- Review the previous week's stanza(s), then introduce the new one.

- Try sending a "note" to the music teacher to see if he or she will help out with the music to the song.

- Have copies of the song made for each student.

- Write out a copy on an easel for easy viewing.

- Once the students know the song, make a copy on a cassette or videotape. They love to hear themselves and it makes a nice introduction for next year's lesson!

- If you can't sing, ask your music teacher to tape a copy of the song and the words for you to play for the students.

- This musical memory song won't work for all students, but it's just one more way to reinforce the Dewey numbers.

 Bring a stuffed dog to the library and allow students to check out "Dewey Dog" if they memorize and perform the song!

Pamela Bacon

# THE DEWEY SONG
(to the tune of "Row, Row, Row Your Boat")

Read, read, read a book,
or encyclopedia,
dictionary, almanac,
in zero to 99, ah!

Read, read, read a book,
on philosophy,
behaving, or psychology,
the 100s is where they'll be!

Read, read, read a book,
on religion,
bible stories, mythology,
200s is the region!

Read, read, read a book,
on sociology,
education, manners,
300s even have a fairy!

Read, read, read a book,
about languages foreign,
Spanish, French, Russian, German,
400s is where they're in!

Read, read, read a book,
about all types of science,
biology, zoology, botany, chemistry,
500s start to make sense.

Read, read, read a book,
about the useful arts,
cookbooks, sewing, pets, and health,
600s is where to start.

Read, read, read a book,
about the fine arts,
music, paintings, games, and sports,
700s can teach you darts!

Read, read, read a book,
on literature,
plays, poems, and great authors,
800s the number for sure!

Read, read, read a book,
on geography,
history, history, history, history,
900s is the place to be!

Read, read, read a book,
on any number above,
if you want a nonfiction book,
there's surely one you'll love!

Read, read, read a book,
nonfiction is the game,
fiction, fiction, fiction, fiction,
is found by the last name!

**Lifesaver Tool 40.1.   The Dewey Song**

# WHEEL
# YOU READ MORE?

The book wheel is a fun way to try to get students to read a variety of books instead of just their old favorites. Offering an incentive is not mandatory, but students might be more motivated to roll into the library in search of different types of books!

## Lifesaver Tips

- The Reading Wheel (Lifesaver Tool 41.1) offers excellent opportunities to tie in with teachers. Much of the material covered in class makes a nice addition to the wheels.

- Award Book Bucks or prizes to the first five students to roll into the library with a completed wheel!

- This activity could easily be done more than once in the same school year as long as different books are used.

- For an easy bulletin board, the wheels could be colored and posted.

- Use the wheel as an introduction to the difference between fiction and nonfiction.

- Students can color in each section as they read the book. If you wish, the actual titles can be written on the back of the handout.

 Hang brightly colored wheels from the library ceiling so more books will roll out!

Pamela Bacon

# READING WHEEL

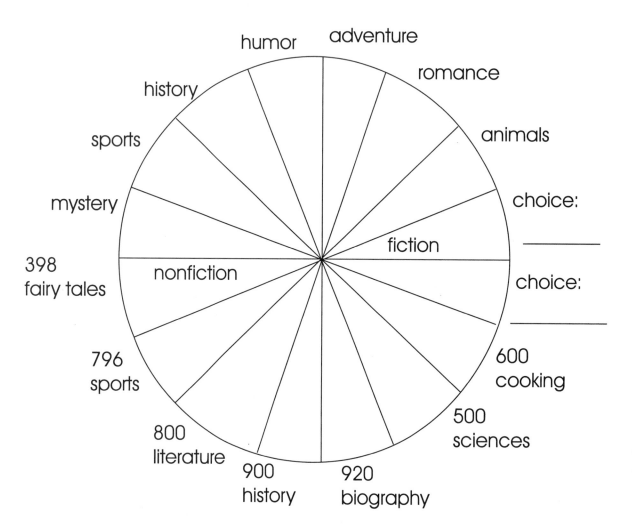

**Lifesaver Tool 41.1.   The Reading Wheel**

# BOOKS YOU WON'T "PART" WITH!

This hands-on activity is a great way to teach students the different parts of a book. The best "part" is that the lesson is great with all elementary grades because you can vary the difficulty level to suit all learners.

## Lifesaver Tips

- Students in grades K–1 can simply color the Parts of a Book Handout (Lifesaver Tool 42.1).

- Students in grades 2–3 can complete the entire activity (as shown on handout).

- Students in grades 4–6 can complete the entire activity and write a summary of their favorite books on the back!

- The completed books look great hanging from the ceiling or on a media-center bulletin board.

 When your big books become too many to leave in one stack, buy plastic laundry hampers. Big books fit in them perfectly and are easier to organize. Teachers love this!

Donna Luther, Media Specialist,
Southmore Intermediate School,
Pasadena, TX

# PARTS OF A BOOK

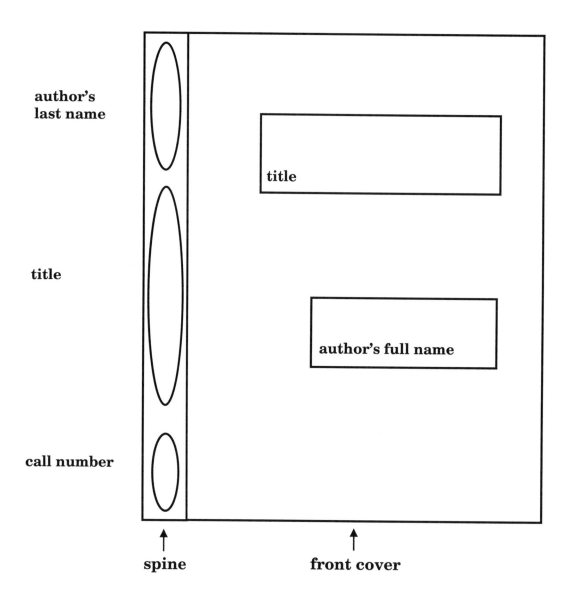

Choose your favorite book and fill in the information for each shape! When you finish, illustrate and color your book cover!

**Lifesaver Tool 42.1.** **Parts of a Book Handout**

From *100 Library Lifesavers.* © 1999 Libraries Unlimited. (800) 237-6124.

# FIND FROGGIE!

This fun learning game is one students will hop into the library to play! (Lifesaver Tool 43.1. Find Froggie Game Questions) Because the activity *is* such fun, students don't even realize they're learning important library skills. So, what are you waiting for? Hop to it!

## Lifesaver Tips

- Divide students into five groups. Students can choose their own groups or, which is easier, assign students to groups when they come into the media center.

- Give each group an envelope with five questions.

- Students must work cooperatively using clues to find five mystery books.

- When students locate the correct book, there will be a frog in the pocket (or back) of the book.

- The first group to find all five frogs wins!

- Tell students you will deduct "frogs" if the group is too noisy or does not work together. This helps control the noise level and encourages participation from all group members.

- I have included five sets of Find Froggie questions for the first game; questions just need to be transferred to index cards. If desired, cards can be laminated for longer use.

- Older students could easily make up clues for younger students if you'd like to play again!

- I have tried to make the questions suitable for all media centers. Before beginning this activity, however, assign a student helper to make sure your library has all the books.

- Ask a student helper to write down the call numbers so you'll have the answers before starting the game.

 For a fun read-aloud that will make students hop into the library, read aloud a chapter from Ellen Conford's *The Frog Princess of Pelham*. (Amazon.com at $11.17.)

Pamela Bacon

# FIND FROGGIE GAME QUESTIONS

## GROUP 1 QUESTIONS:

Q:  A dictionary for first-time students

A:  Call number: _____

Q:  A book by Lindgren

A:  Call number: _____

Q:  A fairy tale about a wolf, a grandmother, and a young girl

A:  Call number: _____

Q:  A book by E. B. White about a pig

A:  Call number: _____

Q:  A biography about Helen Keller

A:  Call number: _____

## GROUP 2 QUESTIONS:

Q:  A book by Coleridge about ships

A:  Call number: _____

Q:  A dictionary by Webster

A:  Call number: _____

Q:  A book of silly poems by Silverstein

A:  Call number: _____

**(Livesaver Tool 43.1 continues on page 132.)**

Q:   A book about hurricanes by Helm

A:   Call number: _____

Q:   The first boxcar children book by G. Chandler Warner

A:   Call number: _____

## GROUP 3 QUESTIONS:

Q:   A joke book featuring Garfield

A:   Call number: _____

Q:   A book by Beverly Cleary about a dog

A:   Call number: _____

Q:   The life story of Helen Keller

A:   Call number: _____

Q:   A book on the life of Anne Frank

A:   Call number: _____

Q:   A book full of synonyms

A:   Call number: _____

## GROUP 4 QUESTIONS:

Q:   A Newbery book by Paula Fox

A:   Call number: _____

Q:   A Peanuts book

A:   Call number: _____

Q:   A book on sign language

A:   Call number: _____

Q:   A Judy Blume fiction book

A:   Call number: _____

Q:   A book on how to raise a puppy

A:   Call number: _____

## GROUP 5 QUESTIONS:

Q:   A biography of Babe Ruth

A:   Call number: _____

Q:   Stories about Sherlock Holmes

A:   Call number: _____

Q:   A book by Louisa May Alcott about girls

A:   Call number: _____

Q:   A book by Shel Silverstein about a special tree

A:   Call number: _____

Q:   A fiction book about pirates by Stevenson

A:   Call number: _____

**Lifesaver Tool 43.1.   Find Froggie Game Questions**

# "STATE" OF MIND

Because this project is somewhat lengthy, you might want to team up with a teacher on this one. Reference skills, writing skills, and geography skills are all wrapped up into one great unit. Your "state" of mind will improve when you see students learning valuable research skills—and enjoying it!

## Lifesaver Tools

- Gather enough manila file folders for each student. These are the students' project folders.

- Ask students to pick a state to research. If they wish, students can draw state names.

- Students begin by gathering books about their home state.

- When the initial research is completed, tell students to use their books to gain ideas on how to decorate their folders.

- Students now write letters to their assigned State Tourism Office. In the letters, students ask the office to send them information. (Lifesaver Tool 44.2. Sample Letter to State Tourism Office Handout)

- Use your library's latest edition of the *World Almanac and Book of Facts* to obtain all the addresses.

- Older students can use the *World Almanac and Book of Facts* to find their own addresses!

- After decorating their folders and writing their letters of inquiry, students now research their states in more depth as they follow along on the handy to-do list. (Lifesaver Tool 44.3. State Research Project Checklist Handout)

- If teaming with a teacher, the students earn points based on their project folders. See Lifesaver Tool 44.1 (Project Folder Form) for a breakdown of points.

 Are you in a "state" of confusion about a good bulletin board idea? Post a U.S. map on the bulletin board and surround it with letters from each state as they arrive. If you use a brightly colored fabric instead of paper, the backing should last all year!

Pamela Bacon

# WHAT A STATE YOU'RE IN!

Folder Decoration                 _____ 10 points

Letter of Inquiry                 _____ 20 points

Information Received              _____ bonus points

Research                          _____ 20 points


50 points—TOTAL

· · · · · · · · · · · · · · · · · · · · · · · · · · · · · · · · · · · · · · · · · · · · · · · · · ·

# WHAT A STATE YOU'RE IN!

Folder Decoration                 _____ 10 points

Letter of Inquiry                 _____ 20 points

Information Received              _____ bonus points

Research                          _____ 20 points


50 points—TOTAL

**Lifesaver Tool 44.1.   Project Folder Form**

# SAMPLE LETTER
# TO STATE TOURISM OFFICE

(DATE)

Department of Commerce Visitors Inquiry (SAMPLE ADDRESS)
126 Van Buren Street
Tallahassee, FL 32399-2000

To Whom It May Concern: (SALUTATION)

    I would like to visit your state in the near future. Would you please send me some information regarding places to visit, where to stay, and any other useful information?

    Thank you in advance for your help. I look forward to visiting Florida!
(BODY OF LETTER)

Sincerely, (CLOSING)

John Doe (YOUR NAME)
R. R. 1, Box 000 (RETURN ADDRESS)
Anywhere, IN

**Lifesaver Tool 44.2.**   **Sample Letter to State Tourism Office Handout**

# STATE RESEARCH
# PROJECT CHECKLIST

_____1.   Choose a state to research. State: _____

_____2.   Find an encyclopedia article about your state and briefly scan
          through the information.

_____3.   Decorate your folder to go with your state.

_____4.   Write a letter to your state's tourism office (see sample letter).
          Use the *World Almanac and Book of Facts* to find your inside
          address.

_____5.   Use at least three (3) sources to answer the following questions
          about your state:

    1.   What is the state flower?

    2.   Where is a good place to visit?

    3.   Are there any presidents from your state?

    4.   What is the weather/climate like in December?

    5.   Write down titles of sources used below. Keep all notes
        in your project folder.

    Sources:

    1. _____

    2. _____

    3. _____

**Lifesaver Tool 44.3.   State Research Project Checklist Handout**

From *100 Library Lifesavers.* © 1999 Libraries Unlimited. (800) 237-6124.

# PAT YOURSELF ON THE BACK!

This simple self-assessment allows you to celebrate your job successes and see for yourself where you might want to make some changes. (Lifesaver Tool 45.1. Media Specialist Self-Evaluation Form) Best of all, no one else needs to know how you scored!

## Lifesaver Tips

- Be honest with yourself. Don't answer the way you think you should answer—answer how you really feel!

- Don't take the self-assessment when you've had a bad day—the scores would probably be exaggerated!

- Check over the questions you marked "never" or "sometimes." There may be good reasons for the answers. You may, however, want to readjust if you feel it is justified.

- If you have a buddy who is also a media specialist, talk over your answers.

- If you feel changes can be made, form an action plan to get started on making those changes.

- If there are circumstances that you can't change (hiring a full-time assistant, for example), can you brainstorm some solutions with which you can live?

- Don't be too hard on yourself. Only another media specialist can really understand what an enormous undertaking this job really is!

- The last question is the most important. Really think about this one!

If you feel comfortable with your evaluator, you may want to discuss this self-evaluation with him or her at your annual conference.

 Don't forget to take time for a relaxing cup of hot chocolate on a busy morning. You'll feel better—inside and out!

Pamela Bacon

# MEDIA SPECIALIST SELF-EVALUATION

A = Always      M = Most of the Time      S = Sometimes      N = Never

1. _____ Do you enjoy going to work each day?
2. _____ Do you take at least two short breaks daily?
3. _____ Do you feel you are good at your job?
4. _____ Are you constantly thinking of new activities?
5. _____ Is your media center neat and organized?
6. _____ Is your media center warm and inviting?
7. _____ Do students and teachers often come to visit?
8. _____ Do your administrators visit occasionally?
9. _____ Is the noise level productive or just noisy?
10. _____ Is discipline a concern in the media center?
11. _____ Are students usually focused and on task?
12. _____ Is the media center often reserved by teachers?
13. _____ Do you feel comfortable working with the teachers?
14. _____ Are you comfortable handling administrative tasks?
15. _____ Is your budget orderly and balanced?
16. _____ Do you sponsor any groups or extracurriculars?
17. _____ Do you model reading for pleasure and information?
18. _____ Is your audiovisual room neat and orderly?
19. _____ Do all teachers know AV checkout procedures?
20. _____ Do you regularly attend conferences/workshops?
21. _____ Are you up-to-date on professional resources?
22. _____ Do you communicate with staff about new books?
23. _____ Do your student assistants have a structured plan?
24. _____ Is your library aide on task and helpful?
25. _____ If you had another job option, would you take it?

**Lifesaver Tool 45.1.**    **Media Specialist Self-Evaluation Form**

# GO HOME WITH AN AUTHOR!

Okay, you don't really get to visit these authors' homes, but you can visit their home pages on the Internet (see table 46.1). They're great places for you and your students to visit, but you probably wouldn't want to live there!

## Lifesaver Tips

- Before turning the students loose on the Internet, give a few lessons and guidelines on using it.

- Discuss Internet vocabulary, such as *search engine, home page,* and *http address.*

- Instruct students as to where they can (and can't!) go.

- Demonstrate how to find two or three good search engines.

- Demonstrate how to type in an http address manually.

- Set a time limit for students.

- Pair students up to give more students a chance to use the Internet.

- For best results, bookmark only those sites that you want students to visit.

- Make a schedule for students. (Lifesaver Tool 46.1. Sign-Up Schedule)

- Have parents sign a permission slip, if needed, allowing students access to the Internet. Schools have different policies on this new technology, so be sure to check with your administration before planning Internet lessons.

- Select a different Internet site to highlight each library visit. Keep a log (or write in your plan book) so that you know where you've been!

- Five wonderful home page addresses for authors (and characters!) are as follows:

**Table 46.1.  Go Home with an Author or Character**

| Jan Brett | http://www.janbrett.com |
|---|---|
| Tomie dePaola | http://www.bingley.com |
| Winnie the Pooh | http://www.penguinputnam.com/yreaders/pooh/winnie.htm |
| Magic School Bus | http://www.scholastic.com/ |
| Awesome Authors on the Web | http://www.jps.net/hatzi/awesomeauthors.htm |

 Ask another teacher to e-mail you during a class. The teacher should pretend to be a book character and give at least three meaningful clues about the book. Challenge the class to identify the mystery character. The tricky part comes when you can only answer "Yes" or "No" to all questions. See how long it takes students to figure out the book character's identity.

Pamela Bacon

# SIGN-UP SCHEDULE

| DATE | NAME | TEACHER/GRADE | TIME ON | TIME OFF | INITIALS |
|------|------|---------------|---------|----------|----------|
|      |      |               |         |          |          |
|      |      |               |         |          |          |
|      |      |               |         |          |          |
|      |      |               |         |          |          |
|      |      |               |         |          |          |
|      |      |               |         |          |          |
|      |      |               |         |          |          |
|      |      |               |         |          |          |
|      |      |               |         |          |          |
|      |      |               |         |          |          |
|      |      |               |         |          |          |
|      |      |               |         |          |          |
|      |      |               |         |          |          |
|      |      |               |         |          |          |
|      |      |               |         |          |          |
|      |      |               |         |          |          |
|      |      |               |         |          |          |
|      |      |               |         |          |          |
|      |      |               |         |          |          |
|      |      |               |         |          |          |
|      |      |               |         |          |          |
|      |      |               |         |          |          |
|      |      |               |         |          |          |
|      |      |               |         |          |          |
|      |      |               |         |          |          |
|      |      |               |         |          |          |
|      |      |               |         |          |          |
|      |      |               |         |          |          |
|      |      |               |         |          |          |
|      |      |               |         |          |          |

# Computer Sign-Up!

**Lifesaver Tool 46.1.**   **Computer Sign-Up Form**

From *100 Library Lifesavers.* © 1999 Libraries Unlimited. (800) 237-6124.

# A LITTLE CONSIDERATION, PLEASE!

I'm thrilled to admit that I've never had a book questioned by a parent, teacher, or administrator. However, if and when that time arises (and I hope it never does!) I have a plan ready. (Lifesaver Tool 47.1. Procedures for Questioned Library Materials Form) Now you can, too.

## Lifesaver Tips

- Have this material neatly photocopied and labeled in a file folder.

- Know where the file is—just in case!

- If you receive a complaint, calmly hand over the information. Try not to get into a discussion about the book. Rather, simply explain the procedures for questioned books.

- Try to remember the person is complaining about the book and not you personally.

- Be courteous.

- Advise your administrator immediately of the concern so that he or she is aware of the potential problem.

- Document the date and time the person came in. Briefly log how you handled the situation and what material was given to the concerned patron.

 If a book is questioned, contact the American Library Association (ALA) immediately! The principal needs to be the first person at your school to know.

Pamela Bacon

# PROCEDURES FOR QUESTIONED LIBRARY MATERIALS

Name _____ Date _____

Phone No. _____ (W) E-mail_____

_____ (H) Fax No._____

Address _____

_____

Title(s) of questioned material _____

_____

Author(s) _____

Specific concerns_____

_____

_____

What is your recommendation for the questioned material?

_____ Not allow circulation for certain grades

_____ Not allow your child to view material

_____ Removal from media center

_____ Other: _____

*Note:* The above question is only to obtain your opinion and/or feedback. It is not necessarily the action that will be taken.

Have you read or viewed the *entire* work in question? _____

Are you familiar with professional reviews of this material?_____

If yes, please indicate the reviewing source or sources._____

_____

Are you familiar with the School Library Bill of Rights? _____

Thank you for your input. Please indicate further action you would like taken at this time:

_____ Telephone call/meeting with principal

_____ Telephone call/meeting with superintendent

_____ Follow-up letter from media specialist

_____ Other: _____

SIGNATURE_____ DATE_____

**Lifesaver Tool 47.1.   Procedures for Questioned Library Materials Form**

# FREEBIES ARE PRICELESS!

With the increasing costs of books, periodicals, and other library materials, the budget for incentives seems to get smaller and smaller each year! The idea of asking for free stuff isn't new at all, but I've included a form letter to make begging just a little easier! (Lifesaver Tool 48.1. Request for Free Materials Form Letter)

## Lifesaver Tips

- Make three file folders.

- Label the first file "WAITING."

- Label the second "NO RESPONSE."

- Label the third file "DONE."

- Make a photocopy of each letter you send. Obviously, the outgoing copies go into the "WAITING" file after mailing.

- When you get a negative response to a letter, file the letter anyway in the "DONE" folder. (This is your reminder not to write to them again!)

- After a designated period, move letters from the "WAITING" file to the "NO RESPONSE" folder.

- For those letters filed under "NO RESPONSE," you can send a second letter later if time allows.

- Each year, go through the "DONE" folder and check for companies who did respond favorably by sending freebies. You may want to ask for their help again if enough time has elapsed.

- As far as the addresses are concerned, a number of great sources are available. *Free Stuff for Kids 1998* is an excellent source. Use the *World Almanac and Book of Facts* to write to businesses or sports teams; they are an excellent source for obtaining free items.

- Older students can type personal letters as part of a library or classroom activity. Obviously, these letters are far more personal and probably more likely to get a quicker response.

- Don't give up—lots of places send free items upon request. You just have to ask—and keep asking!

- I intentionally removed the date so that this letter could be readily photocopied. On your file copy, be sure to write down the date so you'll know how much time has elapsed.

- Because no return address appears on the letter, also be sure your envelope includes your school address, e-mail address, telephone number, and fax number.

 Use posters that come in magazines for giveaways. Chances are, popular teen idols will be torn out by a borrower anyway!

Pamela Bacon

# FROM THE MEDIA CENTER

Greetings! Because you know the importance of reading, we are calling upon you to help. The purpose of this letter is to request your support in obtaining free materials for our school. Our school would appreciate any samples, giveaways, or freebies you could provide. These items will be used as prizes and incentives for classroom and library contests.

Thank you in advance for your contribution. Your help is greatly appreciated and the happiness the students receive is guaranteed to be priceless!

Sincerely,

_____

Media Specialist

**Lifesaver Tool 48.1.   Request for Free Materials Form Letter**

# TO COPY OR NOT TO COPY

One of the biggest parts of our job as library media specialists is knowing if teachers have the right to copy material. There's a lot to know pertaining to copyright laws, so here's all the rights (and wrongs!) of whether you should (or should not!) copy. (Lifesaver Tool 49.1. Fair Use of Copyrighted Material Handout)

## Lifesaver Tips

- When in doubt, write for permission!

- The main rule applying to education is that, in most cases, teachers may not use more than 10 percent of a work without permission.

- Nonprofit, educational uses are considered fair use in many cases.

- When copying money (for Book Bucks or other uses), the copying must be done in black and white (no color!), about half the original size, and plates (originals) must be destroyed after use.

- You may make multiple copies of a poem if it is shorter than 250 words.

- You may take an excerpt from a poem, but no more than 250 words.

- No copying of consumables (e.g., workbooks) may be done!

- The same item may not be copied from term to term without permission.

- *Fair use* means one time only!

- Teachers may make a single copy of a chapter, article, poem, or story—but not multiple copies!

- Taping may be done from the air (not cable) for instructional use.

- Programs must be used within 10 days and erased within 45 days!

- Workbook pages may not be made into transparencies without permission.

- A student may tape a record for a class presentation, but a teacher may not!

- Linworth Publishing's *Copyright for School Libraries: A Practical Guide* by Carol Mann Simpson is a good source to read and then pass on to others.

---

 Post an easy-to-read, laminated poster of copyright laws for teachers over the copier. If teachers choose to break the rules, they can't say you haven't told them!

Pamela Bacon

---

# FAIR USE: A RECAP

## WHEN IS A USE OF COPYRIGHTED MATERIAL A "FAIR USE"?: A RECAP

### THE FOUR-FACTOR ANALYSIS:

### (1) WHAT IS THE PURPOSE AND CHARACTER OF THE USE?

A nonprofit, educational use is more likely to be fair than a commercial use, but it is not determinative. A not-for-profit student publication can still infringe a copyright. Political or social commentary is also more likely to be fair use.

### (2) WHAT IS THE NATURE OF THE COPYRIGHTED WORK?

Use of a work closer to the "core" of copyright is less likely to be fair than use of a work at the fringe of copyright's protection. Works containing a high degree of factual material from the public domain are farther from the copyright core than works containing mostly creative and original material.

### (3) HOW MUCH OF THE COPYRIGHTED WORK IS USED?

The amount of the work used must be no more than is reasonably necessary to accomplish the fair use. Considering the guidelines for educational use, less than 10 percent of a work is more likely to constitute a fair use than more than 10 percent of the work.

### (4) WHAT IS THE POTENTIAL EFFECT OF THE USE ON THE MARKET FOR THE ORIGINAL?

If consumers are willing to buy the use as a substitute for the original, then the use is probably not fair. One should also consider the potential effect on the market for the original if uses like the one at issue were to become widespread.

Reprinted by permission from *Law of the Student Press*, Second edition. Arlington, VA: Student Press Law Center, 1994.

**Lifesaver Tool 49.1.   Fair Use of Copyrighted Material Handout**

# WHAT'S NEW?

A handout letting staff know about new materials certainly isn't new in itself, but the fact that it's ready to be photocopied and used might be, and being able to find it when you want to might be new as well. (Lifesaver Tool 50.1. What's New in the Media Center Handout)

## Lifesaver Tips

- Run the form off on bright paper! That way, it's less likely to get lost in the teacher's mailbox.

- I send a copy of this form to any teacher who asks me to purchase a book, magazine, or other item for the library. It's a simple gesture, but shows the teacher that you followed through on the request. Chances are, the teacher may even have forgotten he or she asked for it, but it's nice to let that person know that *you* didn't.

- In some cases, you could check the item out to the teacher and place this form in the item.

- If the material is unavailable, send a short note to the requesting teacher to let him or her know of your efforts, however unsuccessful!

- This procedure is especially helpful for naysayers. You might never change their attitude about the media center, but even negative teachers appreciate a little extra effort!

⫸ When new books arrive, book an informal party—no reservations required!

Pamela Bacon

# WHAT'S NEW IN THE MEDIA CENTER?

## *COME IN AND SEE!*

TO:

FROM:

Greetings from the Media Center!

We have purchased the following material you requested:

_____

_____

The material is now ready and can be checked out at any time.

You can find the item(s) at _____.

Thanks for your help in choosing materials for our school Media Center!

**Lifesaver Tool 50.1.   What's New in the Media Center Handout**

# 50 NIFTY TIPS TO IMPROVE PUBLIC RELATIONS

Whether we like it or not, public relations opportunities in the media center are something we can't afford to lose. With the tightening budgets and staffing cutbacks going on in media centers nationwide, good PR skills are no longer an asset, but a requirement. (Lifesaver Tool 51.1. 50 Nifty Tips to Improve Public Relations)

## Lifesaver Tips

- If you don't receive support from your local newspaper editor right away, keep trying. Editors are extremely busy people who are usually willing to help. The trick is, you have to catch them!

- Don't try to implement more than five PR strategies each year. It's better to be consistent and follow through than to try a lot of new ideas you can't keep up with.

- Celebrate summer and renew yourself.

- If you try the journal idea, be sure it doesn't fall into the wrong hands—such as a student's or principal's!

- Be sure to get permission before bringing live animals to school— I learned this the hard way!

- Encourage your staff to model reading by having popular adult fiction and nonfiction books available to trade.

- If a student booktalks a book, other students will listen better than they ever will to you (sad but true!).

- If you really want to win teachers over, take a computer trouble-shooting class and offer assistance anytime you can.

- Trade places with your principal for a day—what an eye-opener for both of you!

- Ask for parent volunteers to help with your newsletter.

 Librarians and teachers don't often take time to celebrate their successes. I purchase a pack of party horns at the beginning of each year to give to my staff. That way, they'll be more likely to "toot their own horns!"

Tamora K. Brewer, Assistant Principal,
Tzouanakis Intermediate School,
Greencastle, IN

# 50 NIFTY TIPS TO IMPROVE PUBLIC RELATIONS

- Take pictures regularly and send them to the local newspaper.
- Write and send home a monthly newsletter.
- Host open library nights one evening a week.
- Form a Friends of the Library Club.
- Join your local teachers group and rally for media specialists.
- Write grants every time you get the chance.
- Serve coffee, newspapers, and quiet time for teachers and administrators on weekday mornings.
- Put bookmarks in your staff mailboxes.
- Volunteer to shelve books at your local library.
- Host an annual book sale.
- Introduce yourself to each school board member.
- Produce an annual report and distribute it to your superintendent and principal.
- Buy a blank journal and pass it back and forth between teachers for jokes and funny anecdotes.
- Bring in a different pet each month.
- Each week, send a nice note to a different staff member.
- Join the school's technology committee!
- Meet annually with the curriculum director.
- Get on your school's social committee.
- Be positive about your school and your library!
- Write articles for publication—then toot your own horn!
- Start a brown-bag reading club at lunch for students.
- Wear fun promotional T-shirts and sweatshirts.
- Get out of the library and into the teacher's lounge!
- Attend every school board meeting—make a presentation at least once yearly.
- Have a library action plan and goals. Post and share them!
- Invite local celebrities to come in and talk to students. Take pictures!

**(Lifesaver Tool 51.1 continues on page 160.)**

- Provide a note of support for teachers having a bad day!
- Make yourself indispensable!
- Use substituting as an opportunity to promote career awareness. Have career-related videos and activities on hand.
- Offer a laminating service for teachers on Fridays.
- Provide a copy service (mine is called *Pages*) for students. Use fees generated to buy books for the library.
- Host authors' visits any time you can.
- Offer preview videos to overworked teachers as a break for them (and you!).
- Really listen to students and hear what they have to say.
- Help out with the school play—it's a joy to see students involved in reading!
- Take tickets at ball games while wearing a library sweatshirt. Pass out *Reading Is a Ball* buttons.
- Set up regular dinner meetings each month for all local librarians.
- Attend and participate in as many professional meetings as your time allows.
- Become an active member of local, state, and regional library organizations.
- Keep a scrapbook of reading-related news articles and photographs.
- Support local charities by making small donations from your overdue book funds.
- Take one day off each year to do nothing but read a good book.
- Post a different reading-related quote each week on your library's home page.
- Publish a regular book review column in your school newspaper (or better yet, offer to edit student-written columns).
- Use morning announcements as booktalk opportunities with students.
- Support your school by purchasing items from every fund-raiser.
- As hard as it is, always be nice to salespeople who call.
- Be prepared and ready to assist teachers with computer problems.
- Make it a rule not to gossip about teachers—this bad habit can damage public relations more quickly than you can open your mouth!
- Model reading at every opportunity.

**Lifesaver Tool 51.1.   Tips to Improve Public Relations**

# GET IN ON THE ACTION!

Whenever you turn around these days, it seems as though there's a new self-help book out on meeting your goals or writing action plans. This lifesaver just gives you the basic steps needed to form your own action plan. (Lifesaver Tool 52.1. Library Action Plan) Although designed for your school, it could just as easily be a start to your personal action plan. Hey, if you want more on the subject, just go to your local library and check out any of Stephen Covey's books. I bet you know where to find them!

## Lifesaver Tips

- An action plan isn't essential, but it sure helps by adding a commitment to make positive changes.

- Although an action plan can be implemented at any time during the school year, the beginning of the school year is ideal.

- If your time line isn't met, don't give up. Perhaps your time line wasn't reasonable or other changes became more important.

- Continue to revise your action plan as needed to reflect your changing vision for your media center.

Read Stephen Covey's *First Things First* and Kenneth Blanchard's *The One Minute Manager. The One Minute Manager Meets the Monkey* (also by Blanchard) is also a great one to help you get the monkey off your back!

Pamela Bacon

# GET IN ON THE ACTION:
# FIVE STEPS TO
# WRITING A LIBRARY ACTION PLAN!

1. Collect evidence. List three things that show you changes should be made.

2. List three people you could work with to create a shared vision statement for the future of your media center.

3. Write the vision statement for your media center. How will you share these changes with others?

4. What are three things you can do to make these changes a reality? What are some ways you can make sure positive changes continue to improve?

5. Develop a time line for the major changes in your vision statement. Provide suggested dates for when changes should be implemented.

**Lifesaver Tool 52.1.** **Library Action Plan**

# TO BUY OR NOT TO BUY

Choosing materials for the media center is never an easy task, especially when budgets keep getting smaller and smaller. With the costs of books continually on the rise, you can never be too careful. Here's a handy form to help you decide to buy or not to buy. (Lifesaver Tool 53.1. Book-Buying Safety Form)

## Lifesaver Tips

- Don't be pressured into buying materials from the salesperson who just "happens" to be in the neighborhood.

- If the book is not one that was specifically requested (and time allows), ask teachers for their opinions before purchasing.

- Student feedback before purchasing is also helpful.

- Small presses (the underdogs) sometimes have excellent materials and, because they're smaller, often try harder to please.

- As sad as it is, books (especially fiction) are often judged by their covers. If the cover does not generate interest, you may want to think twice.

- Before purchasing nonfiction books each year, try to get a general idea about which area is most in need of new material; simply scanning each nonfiction section is one way. Do the covers and spines appear worn? Then choose three books at random. What are the copyright dates? This strategy is most helpful for the new media specialist. If you've been there a while, you know which sections need updating.

 Even though many companies allow and even encourage it, never buy books on an empty budget!

Pamela Bacon

# CPR: BOOK-BUYING SAFETY FORM

Title: _____ Type:   E    F    NF    R

Author: _____ Reading Level: _____

Copyright Date: _____ Price: _____

Publisher: _____ Paperback/Hardback: _____

## C = CONTENT

| | | | | |
|---|---|---|---|---|
| 1. | The book is accurate. | Y | N | N/A |
| 2. | The book is current. | Y | N | N/A |
| 3. | The book is well organized. | Y | N | N/A |
| 4. | The writing style is fluent. | Y | N | N/A |
| 5. | The overall book quality is high. | Y | N | N/A |

## P = PHYSICAL ATTRIBUTES

| | | | | |
|---|---|---|---|---|
| 1. | The cover design is attractive. | Y | N | N/A |
| 2. | The font/print is appropriate. | Y | N | N/A |
| 3. | Back of book summary is exciting. | Y | N | N/A |
| 4. | The inside illustrations are good. | Y | N | N/A |
| 5. | The length is appropriate. | Y | N | N/A |

## R = READER CONSIDERATIONS

| | | | | |
|---|---|---|---|---|
| 1. | Students have requested book. | Y | N | N/A |
| 2. | Teachers have requested book. | Y | N | N/A |
| 3. | Book itself would draw attention. | Y | N | N/A |
| 4. | Contents page/index easy to follow. | Y | N | N/A |
| 5. | Level of difficulty appropriate. | Y | N | N/A |

**Lifesaver Tool 53.1.   Book-Buying Safety Form**

From *100 Library Lifesavers.* © 1999 Libraries Unlimited. (800) 237-6124.

# BIRTHDAY BOOK BASH

Well, a book doesn't taste as good as candy or cake, but it definitely lasts longer. By encouraging parents to purchase books in honor of their child's birthday, everyone celebrates whenever the book is checked out! Plus, new books dot the library shelves. This way the library can have its cake and read it, too!

## Lifesaver Tips

- Before each school year begins, make a collection of birthday posters to post outside the classroom door when a birthday book boy or girl celebrates the big day.

- Laminate the birthday posters for lasting use.

- Teaming with the art teacher on the posters is an excellent way to get creative students' work on display.

- Leave a spot on each poster to place a name (removable) for the birthday child.

- At the beginning of each school year, distribute letters and forms. (Lifesaver Tool 54.1. Birthday Book-Bash Letter; Lifesaver Tool 54.2. Birthday Book-Bash Form) The forms can be returned either during the child's birthday month or by a designated due date to prevent forms from being forgotten or lost.

- Purchase a variety of library plates or stamps to record birthday book information (available through DEMCO 1-800-356-1200).

- Have a "favorite books" list photocopied and ready when parents need book suggestions.

- Take the child's picture with the birthday sign and book. Place pictures in your library newsletter.

- Have students autograph their books below the nameplate for an added thrill.

- Submit birthday book students and pictures each month to the local newspaper.

 On your birthday, buy a special book and donate it to the library—students don't even need to know how young you are!

Pamela Bacon

# BIRTHDAY BOOK-BASH LETTER

Dear Parents:

I would like to remind you of the Birthday Book-Bash program at our school.

The purpose of this special program is to promote birthdays, reading, and books all at the same time.

Here's how the Birthday Book-Bash program works:

1.  Choose a book you wish to purchase in honor of your child's birthday. You may discuss the choice with your child or let it be a surprise.

2.  If you need help choosing a title, let me know. I will be happy to help you choose the perfect birthday book. The main thing is to choose one of your child's favorites.

3.  Fill out the Birthday Book-Bash Form. Return it to school by

    _____.

4.  The book will have a nameplate stamped just inside the front cover in honor of your child's book dedication.

5.  On your child's birthday, the book will be displayed along with a Happy Birthday poster outside the classroom door. In addition, your child gets to borrow the book first!

6.  Summer birthdays can be honored any time you choose!

Feel free to contact me if you have questions or comments.

Sincerely,

_____

Media Specialist

**Lifesaver Tool 54.1.   Birthday Book-Bash Letter**

# BIRTHDAY BOOK-BASH FORM

Student's Name: _____

Date of Birth: _____ Grade: _____

Homeroom Teacher: _____

I would like to order one of the following birthday books:

Choice 1: _____

Choice 2: _____

(Second choice will be used only if first choice is out of print or unavailable.)

Please enclose payment of $10 with your order.

Checks should be made payable to: _____.

You will receive a receipt shortly. Thanks so much for participating in our birthday book program!

Sincerely,

Media Specialist

# HUNT FOR A GREAT BOOK!

Hunting is always in season in the media center. For best results, however, I don't recommend this activity at the end of the school year, due to the unstructuredness and high energy level associated with the activity. But, do use this activity any other time you're hunting for a fun lesson!

## Lifesaver Tips

- For best results, don't do the hunt more than once or twice in the same day (otherwise, the school may have to hunt for a new media specialist!).

- Tell students all forms should be neatly and completely filled out. Otherwise, the student(s) will be disqualified and lose his or her hunting license!

- Students should use the card catalog to find a hunting book of each type: fiction, reference, easy, and nonfiction.

- After locating a hunting book of each type, students should locate the book on the shelf and record the information requested on the handout.

- Books should be returned to the shelf in their proper place or else students will be asked to hunt for them!

- I chose the theme of hunting for an all-purpose theme. The theme could easily be varied as desired.

## Procedures

- Distribute a handout to each student. (Lifesaver Tool 55.1. Hunting License Handout)

- Divide students into teams of four or fewer students.

- Start each team at a different section of the library (fiction, reference, easy, nonfiction) for congestion and traffic-flow purposes.

- Students should work together in teams to complete the handout.

- Each team that turns in a completed handout receives a hunting license ticket.

- Five hunting license tickets will be drawn from a box. These five students will be able to hunt through a catalog for a great new book to keep!

- For extra motivation, offer a reward at the hunt's end.

Follow-up questions to be used at the end of the hunt:

1. What is the difference between fiction and nonfiction call numbers?

2. Which of the above are make-believe?

3. What types of books are in the reference area?

4. How are easy/children's books arranged?

 For a new twist, try an Internet scavenger hunt! It's a great way to get students' feet wet while learning Internet skills.

Pamela Bacon

# HUNTING LICENSE

## YOUR TICKET TO UNCOVERING GREAT BOOKS!

Name: _____

Teacher: _____ Grade: _____

```
┌─────────────┐
│    start    │
└─────────────┘

  reference books
  title: _____
  _____
  call #: _____

                        fiction books
                        title: _____
                        author: _____
                        call #: _____

  rest area:
  stop hunting and
  write down sign-out
  procedures on back!

  easy books
  call #: _____
  author: _____
  title: _____
  _____
                        nonfiction books

                        author: _____
                        title: _____
                        call #: _____

┌─────────────┐
│   finish    │
└─────────────┘
```

**Lifesaver Tool 55.1.   Hunting License Handout**

# PICTURE THIS!

Cameras are an easy way to bring fun and excitement into the library. There aren't very many kids who don't like to ham it up for the camera! Although it's often hard to find the time with busy schedules, pictures, as they say, are worth a thousand words!

## Lifesaver Tips

- It's easy to remember to take photos at important events, like open house or when an author visits. It's not so easy to remember to take pictures of students during everyday, mundane events. However, these candid shots of students' reading materials tucked into their book bags or sharing a book together are wonderful keepsakes for your media center mementos book.

- Display new pictures each month on your media center bulletin board. Students love looking at pictures—even when it's not them!

- Send a press release (Lifesaver Tool 56.1. Press Release Form) with pictures regularly to your local newspaper—often editors are looking for pictures with a local flare to fill up space.

- Adding pictures to your library newsletter is an excellent way to gain interest in your publication.

• Take photos of staff members reading—it's a great way to model the joy of reading for students.

• At the end of the year, keep the special photos for your mementos book. Sell the rest for $1 each to students and staff members. This is a great fund-raiser and takes very little effort.

 Be picture perfect! Use Clark Photo Labs (P.O. Box 96300, Washington, DC 20077-7195) to develop your pictures. The prices and fast service (let alone the convenient postage-free mailer) will give you something to smile about!

Pamela Bacon

# PRESS RELEASE FORM

FROM THE MEDIA CENTER

Date: _____

For more information, contact:

Media Specialist: _____

Phone: _____ Fax: _____

Dear Editor:

Please publish the following media center information in your newspaper:

_____

_____

_____

_____

_____

_____ I am enclosing _____ photos.

    Cutline information:

    Names/ages: _____

    Date of event: _____

    Teacher's name (if student): _____

_____ No photographs are enclosed. If you would like to take photos, please call to arrange a time.

    Thank you for your support. Please contact me if you need additional information.

From *100 Library Lifesavers.* © 1999 Libraries Unlimited. (800) 237-6124.

**Lifesaver Tool 56.1.** **Press Release Form**

# MIXED-UP MEDIA CENTER

None of your students will be mixed up about fiction and nonfiction books when this lesson is over! (Lifesaver Tool 57.1. Mixed-Up Media Center Handout)

## Lifesaver Tips

- Before you begin this activity, discuss the difference between fiction and nonfiction.

- As a help to students, I always remind them that *nonfiction* starts with an *n*, and so does *number*. Thus, nonfiction uses numbers. Another helpful hint is that fiction starts with an *f*, and so does the word *fake*. *Fiction* books are all *fakes*!

- This activity could be used as an introduction to the Dewey Decimal System.

- If time allows, students can design their own libraries by adding color and/or illustrations.

- I recommend this activity for grades 4–6.

- For an enrichment activity, ask students to make up book titles and authors' names for the books.

To prevent your media center from becoming mixed up, purchase single-sided shelving when possible. You can always bump them up to each other to make them double-sided, but single-sided shelves can always go against the wall.

Pamela Bacon

# MIXED-UP MEDIA CENTER!

Name: _____

Teacher: _____ Grade: _____

Directions: Help! Overdue, the Library Ghost, came in overnight and left lost books all over the library. Put the books in order on the correct shelf. For the mystery book missing a call number, solve the mystery by adding the correct call number and shelving it. Good luck!

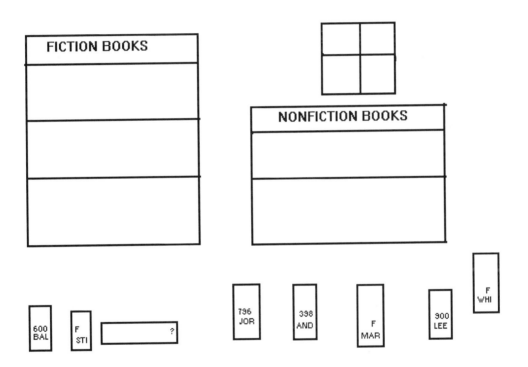

**Lifesaver Tool 57.1.** **Mixed-Up Media Center Handout**

# LOST AND FOUND

We all know the story. It's the end of the year and no matter how much you've hounded those students with overdues, they're still not in yet! Here's a form that's ready to copy and send home to parents. (Lifesaver Tool 58.1. Lost Book Form Letter) You'll be surprised how many books turn up when parents find out how much they cost to replace! With this lifesaver, the only thing you have to lose is lost books.

## Lifesaver Tips

- For best results, mail the letter home instead of giving it to the student to take home.

- Before sending the form home, double-check the shelf to ensure the book isn't there. It's embarrassing when parents call (or worse, come in) and you find out the book was there all along.

- If you know a student doesn't have the money to pay for a book, offer to let him or her work off the lost book by helping out in the library one day after school.

- In the fall, if the books aren't returned or money paid, contact the parents one more time before writing the book off for good.

Does shelving books make you sneeze? There are two possible causes: mold and old! I can't help you with the old, but I can help with the mold. A bleach and water solution is your solution for mold. Use three tablespoons of bleach per one quart of water. Wear rubber gloves and follow cautions as recommended on the bleach bottle. (Strengthen or dilute the mixture as needed, depending on the condition of the books.)

Pamela Bacon

# Lost Book Form Letter

Date: _____

Dear Parent:

This letter is to let you know that your son/daughter did not turn in his/her library books. The item(s) that were not returned are as follows:

TITLE: _____

COST: _____


TITLE: _____

COST: _____


TITLE: _____

COST: _____

If you find the book(s) over the summer, please return them to the school at your earliest convenience. If you do not find the book(s), please mail or bring the money to replace the lost books to the school office. Thanks for your help in locating these missing books. Have a great summer!

Sincerely,

_____

Media Specialist

**Lifesaver Tool 58.1.    Lost Book Form Letter**

# INFORMATION, PLEASE!

Teachers who assign research projects without notifying the media center create one of the most inconvenient aspects of the media specialist's job. This form helps make sure we're all reading off the same page! (Lifesaver Tool 59.1. For Your Information Form)

## Lifesaver Tips

- Photocopy the For Your Information Form and distribute it at the beginning of each school year and second semester.

- For teachers who don't send students down with a form, send one back with the student—perhaps the teacher will get the hint.

- Have a basket of forms in a convenient place for teachers when they visit the media center.

- Public librarians always appreciate receiving a copy of these forms, too!

- Remind teachers that it's easier to know if materials will be available for students if you know the assignment in advance. If two teachers are working on the same topic simultaneously, arrangements can be worked out with a little advance notice.

- If the form is filled out, ask the teacher if he or she would like you to pull thematic materials and deliver them to the classroom for use during the project. This added service takes time, but also lets teachers know you appreciate the advance notice.

 Cruise on over to your telephone and order John D. Volkman's *Cruising Through Research: Library Skills for Young Adults* (Libraries Unlimited 1-800-237-6124). It's a fun way to give students a crash course in library research.

Pamela Bacon

# FOR YOUR INFORMATION!

TEACHER'S NAME: _____

ACTIVITY/PROJECT: _____

_____ I would like to bring my class to the media center for _____ day(s)

beginning _____.

_____ Attached is a student handout.

_____ Assignment Details:

      Date due: _____

      Number of students: _____

      Assignment description: _____

      _____

      _____

_____ My students will need the following library materials:

_____

_____ I would like room materials checked out on the following subject:

_____

_____ My students will/will not need the computers reserved.

**Lifesaver Tool 59.1.** **For Your Information Form**

# WISH LIST

There's nothing special about this form—it's just another tool to help you keep track of possible purchases. (Lifesaver Tool 60.1. Wish List Form) Too bad we can't wish for more library funds!

## Lifesaver Tips

- Photocopy these forms in neon colors to draw attention to them when you place them in staff/administrative mailboxes.

- Keep the forms even if you don't have funds to purchase the items—just in case!

- For organizational purposes, keep forms in the following marked file folders: *To Buy Now* and *To Buy Later*.

- These forms are also useful for you to complete when browsing through your favorite professional magazines.

 "You Can't Scare Me—I Teach!" Find this poster and other hilarious choices in the latest Argus catalog. Argus (1-972-396-6500) specializes in posters for the educational market.

Pamela Bacon

# WISH LIST

Name: _____ Date: _____

I would like the following item(s) to be purchased:

Title: _____

Author (if available): _____

Format (circle one):     Book        Video        Other: _____

Title: _____

Author (if available): _____

Format (circle one):     Book        Video        Other: _____

Title: _____

Author (if available): _____

Format (circle one):     Book        Video        Other: _____

I would like to find more materials in the library on_____

_____

Follow-Up:

_____ Ordered (Date: _____ )

_____ Plan to order (Approximate date: _____ )

_____ Not available/out of print

_____ Kept on file

_____ Did not order (Reason: _____ )

**Lifesaver Tool 60.1.   Wish List Form**

# ARE YOUR STUDENTS *ADEPT* AT USING REFERENCE BOOKS?

This lesson helps students learn to use the following five basic reference tools: A (Almanac), D (Dictionary), E (Encyclopedia), P (Periodical), and T (Thesaurus). When your students have mastered reference tools, you may feel more adept as a media specialist, too! (Lifesaver Tool 61.1. Reference Tools Evaluation and Quiz Form)

## Lifesaver Tips

Before introducing this activity, explain the differences between the tools:

Almanac—includes up-to-date information on a variety of topics. Published each year. Use to find brief facts quickly.

Dictionary—shows spellings, meanings, and pronunciation of words in alphabetical order.

Encyclopedia—includes several books; usually each letter (A–Z) is a different volume. Includes pictures and information about almost every subject. Useful for researching a subject.

Periodical—newspapers and magazines. *Abridged Readers' Guide to Periodical Literature 1998* shows subjects. Periodicals are good for the latest information because they are published daily, weekly, or monthly.

Thesaurus—mainly used to find synonyms for words. Useful in adding variety to writing.

- Have students take notes on why certain tools are better than others in certain situations. Allow notes to be used during the activity.

- Because the *Readers' Guide* is more than a lesson in itself, this activity might provide a nice introduction.

- Because encyclopedias, dictionaries, and many other reference tools are now available electronically, this adds an additional focus to the lesson!

 Search your local bookstore for *Brainstorms and Blueprints: Teaching Library Research as a Thinking Process* (Stripling and Pitts). The resource is geared for grades 7–12 and is available through Libraries Unlimited (1-800-237-6124).

Pamela Bacon

# REFERENCE TOOLS EVALUATION

NAME: _____ TEACHER: _____

### HOW *ADEPT* AT USING REFERENCE TOOLS ARE YOU?

If you've spent any time at all in a library, you know there are thousands of books arranged on the shelves. Well, different kinds of books include different kinds of information. You're now going to learn which book is best for the job!

**A**  Almanac:_____

_____

_____

**D**  Dictionary: _____

_____

_____

**E**  Encyclopedia: _____

_____

_____

**P**  Periodical: _____

_____

_____

**T**  Thesaurus: _____

_____

_____

Now that you're ADEPT with the five reference tools, see if you can choose the right book for the job!

1. Who won the Super Bowl in 1982?
    Best book: _____
    Reason: _____

2. Which is the one you eat? *desert* or *dessert*
    Best book: _____
    Reason: _____

3. What happened to the president yesterday?
    Best book: _____
    Reason: _____

4. Who was president two years ago?
    Best book: _____
    Reason: _____

5. I'm writing a two-page report on Abraham Lincoln.
    Best book: _____
    Reason: _____

6. I need three quick facts about Abraham Lincoln.
    Best book: _____
    Reason: _____

7. What is another word to use for *president* in my report?
    Best book: _____
    Reason: _____

8. Which word is spelled correctly? *judgment* or *judgement*
    Best book: _____
    Reason: _____

9. What will the weather be like tonight?
    Best book: _____
    Reason: _____

10. How do you pronounce *finesse*?
    Best book: _____
    Reason: _____

**Lifesaver Tool 61.1.   Reference Tools Evaluation and Quiz Form**

# THE ABCs OF THE MEDIA CENTER

Learning the ABCs of the media center can be fun for students from kindergarten to sixth grade. (Lifesaver Tool 62.1. Media Center A–Z Form) All that's needed is a little adaptation from you and some creativity (not included!).

## Lifesaver Tips

- For primary grades, do the activity as a group. Use the chalkboard to record the letters.

- Intermediate grades can do the activity on their own, either individually or in small groups.

- Upper-elementary students can write the word and then give an example (Example: A—Atlas, *World Book* Atlas).

- If time allows, students can draw miniature pictures of some of the items.

- This activity can easily be revised. For example, instead of using the letters A–Z, try using different phrases like *Reading Is Fun* or your school's name—the possibilities are endless.

 Looking for some good clean fun? Purchase some sponges in the shapes of letters and allow groups to sponge-paint titles of their favorite books!

Pamela Bacon

# MEDIA CENTER A–Z

NAME: _____TEACHER: _____

Directions: List materials and equipment in the media center that begin with each letter of the alphabet.

A - _____

B - _____

C - _____

D - _____

E - _____

F - _____

G - _____

H - _____

I - _____

J - _____

K - _____

L - _____

M - _____

N - _____

O - _____

P - _____

Q - _____

R - _____

S - _____

T - _____

U - _____

V - _____

W - _____

X - _____

Y - _____

Z - _____

**Lifesaver Tool 62.1.   Media Center A–Z Form**

# DID SOMEONE SAY SURVEY?

If you really want to know how you're doing in your job as a media specialist, forget the principal! Instead, ask your students! (Lifesaver Tool 63.1. Student Survey Form) You really have to be thick-skinned to give a survey to students, but student feedback can be invaluable for the improvement of your media center program.

## Lifesaver Tips

- Don't give a student survey during your first year as a media specialist. Wait until you know the students and the school better.

- As hard as it is, try not to take negative comments personally.

- Obviously, not every comment is accurate. Rather, look for consistency of comments and then concentrate on ways to improve based upon the feedback.

- Consider putting some of the comments in your annual report. If you're trying to get funding for computers, for example, students' comments about the lack of computers could be very helpful.

 Use negative (but honest!) feedback from students as an opportunity to grow.

Pamela Bacon

# STUDENT SURVEY

Name (Optional): _____

Please answer the following questions carefully. Your feedback is important to improve our school media center.

DO YOU USE THE MEDIA CENTER . . .

| | | | |
|---|---|---|---|
| 1. | to complete assignments? | Y | N |
| 2. | to read for enjoyment? | Y | N |
| 3. | to do computer work? | Y | N |
| 4. | to socialize? | Y | N |
| 5. | to get study help? | Y | N |

WOULD YOU LIKE THE MEDIA CENTER TO HAVE MORE . . .

| | | | |
|---|---|---|---|
| 6. | books? If yes, what subjects_____? | Y | N |
| 7. | computers? | Y | N |
| 8. | magazines? | Y | N |
| 9. | videotapes for student checkout? | Y | N |
| 10. | other: _____? | Y | N |

DO YOU . . .

| | | | |
|---|---|---|---|
| 11. | have trouble getting to the media center? | Y | N |
| 12. | think our media center is comfortable? | Y | N |
| 13. | know how to use most equipment/materials? | Y | N |
| 14. | find the media specialist helpful? | Y | N |
| 15. | feel pleased with the media center program? | Y | N |

For any "No" answers, please provide comments below:

Thank you for your comments!

**Lifesaver Tool 63.1.** **Student Survey Form**

# HELP FOR HELPERS!

Because our time is so valuable, we can't waste time with student helpers who don't do what their names implies—help! Carefully interviewing, selecting, and training students, however, can save you time in the long run. If you're looking for helpers, I hope this form "helps"! (Lifesaver Tool 64.1. Student Assistant Application Form)

## Lifesaver Tips

- Intended use: high school. See Lifesaver Tool 38 for junior high/ middle school helpers.

- Even if you're short-handed, try not to hire students unless they are truly qualified.

- Try to hire student helpers early so that they will be able to assist you for a number of years.

- Don't be afraid to let students know that they can be replaced if they don't do what they were hired to do! This can be hard— especially if you really like the student.

- If a student doesn't take the time to complete the application and agree to training, chances are the same student won't follow through as a library helper.

- Be sure to ask for guidance from the student's teacher before hiring an assistant with whom you are not familiar.

- Reward student helpers periodically for their help—they'll work harder when they reap the rewards!

 Use the "three strikes, you're out!" rule with student helpers!

Pamela Bacon

# STUDENT ASSISTANT APPLICATION

Name: _____ Date: _____

Homeroom Teacher: _____ Grade:_____

Address: _____

Phone: _____ Birthday: _____

Hobbies/Interests: _____

Grade Point Average: _____ Attendance Record: _____

What jobs have you held? _____

Please place a check next to areas below that you feel are strengths for you:

_____ Alphabetizing          _____ Filing
_____ Dewey Decimal System   _____ Running Errands
_____ Organization           _____ Following Directions
_____ Neatness

If hired, are you willing to come to an after-school training session? _____

Are you involved in extracurricular activities? _____

If yes, please list: _____

List three references (these may include teachers):

_____

_____

_____

Why do you want to be a student assistant?

_____

Are you available to help before or after school?_____

Please list your current schedule below:

Period 1 _____       Period 5 _____

Period 2 _____       Period 6 _____

Period 3 _____       Period 7 _____

Period 4 _____

Thank you for applying. You will be contacted if you are accepted.

**Lifesaver Tool 64.1.   Student Assistant Application Form**

From *100 Library Lifesavers.* © 1999 Libraries Unlimited. (800) 237-6124.

# HIGH FIVE FOR STUDENT ASSISTANTS

Looking for a good way to evaluate your student helpers? Some schools allow library students to earn credit for hours served. Whether your school allows this or not, it's important for students to be evaluated on their work and performance. (Lifesaver Tool 65.1. Student Assistant Evaluation Form) Usually, scores and motivation are about equal!

## Lifesaver Tips

- If a student scores low in an area, evaluate him or her again after some remediation if you see an effort to improve.

- Discuss the evaluation with the student.

- Even on a poor evaluation, find some reason to give praise as well as constructive criticism.

- Show the evaluation form to students when they apply, so they know right up front what will be expected of them if they are hired.

 A lost student is always more important than a lost book!

Pamela Bacon

# STUDENT ASSISTANT
# EVALUATION FORM

Name: _____ Date: _____

1 = Very Low     2 = Low     3 = Average     4 = High     5 = High+

1.  Attendance                                          _____

2.  Enthusiasm                                          _____

3.  Effort                                              _____

4.  Follows Directions                                 _____

5.  Shows Initiative                                   _____

6.  Neatness                                            _____

7.  Models Good Library Behavior                       _____

8.  Responsible Library User                           _____

9.  Uses Library Equipment Efficiently                 _____

10. Understands and Enforces Library Policies          _____

**Lifesaver Tool 65.1.   Student Assistant Evaluation Form**

# HATS OFF TO YOU!

To be a good media center manager, you must be able to wear a lot of different hats; this library lifesaver concentrates on the five most important hats. (Lifesaver Tool 66.1. Budget Worksheet Form) By changing hats often, your media center will always be in style!

## Lifesaver Tips

### HAT 1   ORGANIZATION

Because of all the different hats you have to wear, organization is critical. Keeping neatly labeled file folders and an organized to-do list are just a few ways to stay organized and keep afloat. If organization is difficult for you, consider reading self-help books, which abound on the subject.

### HAT 2   CREATIVITY

We know the importance of library skills, but many times our students aren't so sure. The best way around this is to create fun, creative lessons so that students don't realize they are really learning important library skills. In addition, be creative about finding ways to collaborate with teachers to teach library skills in conjunction with classroom content. Hats off for team teaching!

### HAT 3   FLEXIBILITY

Flexibility, flexibility, and more flexibility. Whether you've got an exciting lesson planned and a teacher cancels class unexpectedly or your principal asks you to cover a study hall, flexibility is the only answer.

### HAT 4   BUDGETING

School library funds are limited, so it's critical to make the best monetary decisions possible. Plus, it's always embarrassing to be contacted by the central office because your account is overdrawn!

*Note*: The Budget Worksheet is a form to help you prepare your budget. Photocopy it and use it—it makes "cents"!

### HAT 5   CARING

To survive in this profession, you have to care about students first and materials second. You've also got to care enough to want to do the best job possible.

 Ask your local Army recruiter to supply some ball caps for giveaways.

Pamela Bacon

# BUDGET WORKSHEET

| Invoice No. | Company | Item(s) Purchased | Amount | Balance |
|---|---|---|---|---|
| | | | | |
| | | | | |
| | | | | |
| | | | | |
| | | | | |
| | | | | |
| | | | | |
| | | | | |
| | | | | |
| | | | | |
| | | | | |
| | | | | |
| | | | | |
| | | | | |
| | | | | |
| | | | | |
| | | | | |
| | | | | |
| | | | | |
| | | | | |
| | | | | |
| | | | | |
| | | | | |
| | | | | |
| | | | | |
| | | | | |
| | | | | |
| | | | | |
| | | | | |

## Money Makes the Media Center Go 'Round!

**Lifesaver Tool 66.1.** **Budget Worksheet Form**

# X MARKS THE SPOT!

Although this year-long to-do list is designed to help the new media specialist stay afloat in the first-year sea, by transferring the list to a computer, even veteran librarians can benefit by adding their own touches. File the list under X-Files! (Lifesaver Tool 67.1. Year-Long To-Do List)

## Lifesaver Tips

- Take what works from the list and merge it with your own strategies to make a truly individualized year-long to-do list.

- Because it's saved on a computer, you can easily revise it from year to year to keep current.

- Brainstorm with library buddies to form the perfect list.

- Obviously, different facilities have different needs. This lifesaver should help provide a basic framework.

- This lifesaver brings much satisfaction as you continue to cross items off the list!

 Never put more than five things on your daily to-do list!

Pamela Bacon

# YEAR-LONG TO-DO LIST

## BEFORE THE SCHOOL YEAR BEGINS

_____ Review previous year's action plan (Lifesaver 52)

_____ Sort mail (see Lifesaver Tool 99.1)

_____ Revise library policies and rules

_____ Post rules and policies

_____ Photocopy most-used forms

_____ Check equipment inventory—update if needed

_____ Distribute equipment to teachers

_____ Type welcome memo with needed library information

_____ Decorate media center bulletin boards

_____ Hold open house for staff and display new books

_____ Update calendar with the following:

> library classes/times
>
> faculty meetings
>
> after-school events
>
> school events
>
> conferences
>
> extracurricular obligations

_____ Begin signing up classes (if needed)

_____ Hold inservice for library aides and volunteers

_____ Process summer materials

_____ Update budget from summer absence

**(Lifesaver Tool 67.1 continues on page 206.)**

## DURING THE SCHOOL YEAR

_____ Choose and train student assistants

_____ Put up seasonal displays

_____ Send out monthly media center newsletter

_____ Order materials

_____ Read professional literature

_____ Attend conferences and workshops

_____ Work on ongoing inventory (Lifesaver 1)

_____ Team with teachers

_____ Conduct library lessons

## AT THE END OF THE SCHOOL YEAR

_____ Concentrate on overdues

_____ Order materials

_____ Finalize budget figures

_____ Straighten and organize facility

_____ Complete ongoing inventory

_____ Pick up audiovisual equipment

_____ Inventory audiovisual equipment

_____ Arrange special lunch for volunteers

_____ Prepare and submit annual report

_____ Write action plan for next year (Lifesaver 52)

**Lifesaver Tool 67.1.   Year-Long To-Do List**

# CHECK THIS OUT!

This library lifesaver is just a simple form to offer teachers for their classroom libraries. The form includes a place for a date, name, and title when the book is checked out. (Lifesaver Tool 68.1. Classroom Checkout Form) Also included is a place to check off when the book is returned. Teachers appreciate this small, but thoughtful, gesture.

## Lifesaver Tips

- Again, photocopy this form on paper in neon colors and distribute to teachers at the beginning of the school year.

- Photocopy this form again and distribute copies after the Christmas vacation.

 Don't catalog paperbacks! They are often lost and don't have a lasting life. All that's needed is a book pocket and card or barcode label.

Pamela Bacon

# CLASSROOM CHECKOUT FORM

| Name | Title of Book | Date Borrowed | Date Due | Returned |
|------|---------------|---------------|----------|----------|
|  |  |  |  |  |
|  |  |  |  |  |
|  |  |  |  |  |
|  |  |  |  |  |
|  |  |  |  |  |
|  |  |  |  |  |
|  |  |  |  |  |
|  |  |  |  |  |
|  |  |  |  |  |
|  |  |  |  |  |
|  |  |  |  |  |
|  |  |  |  |  |
|  |  |  |  |  |
|  |  |  |  |  |
|  |  |  |  |  |
|  |  |  |  |  |
|  |  |  |  |  |
|  |  |  |  |  |
|  |  |  |  |  |
|  |  |  |  |  |
|  |  |  |  |  |
|  |  |  |  |  |
|  |  |  |  |  |
|  |  |  |  |  |
|  |  |  |  |  |
|  |  |  |  |  |
|  |  |  |  |  |
|  |  |  |  |  |
|  |  |  |  |  |
|  |  |  |  |  |

From *100 Library Lifesavers.* © 1999 Libraries Unlimited. (800) 237-6124.

**Lifesaver Tool 68.1.   Classroom Checkout Form**

# SURF'S UP FOR INTERNET RESEARCH

The Internet is a wonderful tool for research—but only if students know how and when to use it. This lifesaver will help students decide when (and when not) to rely on the Internet for researching purposes. (Lifesaver Tool 69.1. Surf's Up Research Form)

## Lifesaver Tips

**S**  Search for Information

**U**  Use a Narrowed Topic

**R**  Research

**F**  Find Best Information

**S**  Scan Printed Information

**U**  Underline or Highlight Information

**P**  Paraphrase

## Searching Tips

Look for information on your chosen topic using one (or more) of the following search engines:

> http://www.altavista.digital.com/
>
> http://www.webcrawler.com/
>
> http://www.yahoo.com/

Enter a subject.

Look to see how many entries were found.

Look for any hits or good matches.

## Use a Narrowed Topic

Enter a more specific topic.

Check for hits or matches.

If needed, enter a different search term.

> Example: presidents>President Clinton>President Clinton and scandals>President Clinton and Whitewater

## Research

Once you find hits (exact matches), bookmark them.

Choose from 5 to 10 of the best sites.

## Find Best Information

Print out best sites.

Find source of information—is it reliable?

## Scan Printed Information

Scan through information.

Discard unneeded information.

If more material is needed, search Internet further.

## Underline or Highlight Information

Underline or highlight information that supports topic.

Does the information match topic sentence and subject?

Highlight only most important information.

Don't highlight too much information.

## Paraphrase

Paraphrase—put information into own words.

Write paraphrased information on note cards.

Keep track of sources for bibliography.

 Step into research (literally!) with the *Stepping into Research* book. The only step you need to take is to budget $34.95 and call DEMCO (1-800-356-1200).

Pamela Bacon

# SURF'S UP RESEARCH FORM

## AN ORGANIZER FOR INTERNET RESEARCH

Name: _____ Teacher: _____

Assignment Due:_____

    1.   Research topic: _____

    2.   List four possible search terms:

        _____    _____

        _____    _____

    3.   Write down topic sentence below:

        _____

        _____

    4.   List the address for all Web sites used:

        (http://www._____)

        _____

        _____

        _____

        _____

        _____

        _____

**Lifesaver Tool 69.1.**   **Surf's Up Research Form**

# GET THE NUMBER ON AV!

Keeping track of audiovisual information is never easy, but with a lot of organization and a little effort, you can get the number on audiovisual equipment (literally)!

## Lifesaver Tips

- Use the following form to keep track of audiovisual equipment manually. (Lifesaver Tool 70.1. Audiovisual Equipment Form)

- Place forms in a three-ring binder with sections labeled.

- Photocopy form on different-colored sheets of paper. For example, make videotapes pink, audiovisual equipment green, etc.

- If you wish, these forms can be transferred to a computer database.

- Assign each videotape and audiovisual equipment a number. Use a colored-dot label to mark the item so that the number can be seen at a glance. This strategy makes inventory a breeze!

- Make it a point to collect, clean, and assess all audiovisual equipment annually. Even if a teacher uses a videocassette recorder on a permanent loan basis, I still collect it at year's end. This is a subtle reminder that although the teacher has access to it, the equipment still belongs to the media center.

 Need the dirt on a good AV cleaner? To safely clean audiovisual equipment, purchase DEMCO's multimedia cleaning kit (1-800-356-1200).

Pamela Bacon

# AUDIOVISUAL EQUIPMENT FORM

Audiovisual #: _____

Equipment: _____

Model and Brand: _____

_____

Date Purchased: _____   Price: _____

Purchased from: _____

Serial #: _____

Condition:    New              Good              Fair              Poor

Repair Dates: _____

Status: _____

Notes: _____

_____

_____

_____

_____

_____

_____

_____

**Lifesaver Tool 70.1.**   **Audiovisual Equipment Form**

# THE TEN COMMANDMENTS OF SHELVING

Because shelving has become so routine to us, it's sometimes hard to tell someone else how to do it. Use this lifesaver to train student helpers and library volunteers. Hopefully, this lifesaver shalt help get your books in order!

## Lifesaver Tips

- **Commandment 1.** Thou shalt not place books at the back of the shelf (all books should be placed evenly at the front of the shelf).

- **Commandment 2.** Thou shalt not place a book with a number in the fiction section (nonfiction books have numbers and fiction book call numbers have letters).

- **Commandment 3.** Thou shalt not place nonfiction books out of numerical order (see example below):

    100   200   210   210.1   210.21   300   398   398.2   398.29

- **Commandment 4.** Thou shalt not confuse the three letters in the call number (the three letters stand for the first three letters in the author's last name *except* on biographies. On biographies those letters stand for who the book is about—not who wrote it. If a book has no author, those three letters are the first three letters of the title).

- **Commandment 5.** Thou shalt learn library shelving abbreviations: *SC* stands for *story collection*; *F* stands for *fiction*; *E* stands for *easy fiction*; and *B* stands for *biography* (these materials are all shelved separately).

- **Commandment 6.** Thou shalt remind young library users to use shelf markers before removing books from the shelf.

- **Commandment 7.** Thou shalt shelve books regularly (*shelving* means that a returned and carded book is returned to its proper place on the shelf).

- **Commandment 8.** Thou shalt read shelves regularly (*reading shelves* means make sure all books are shelved in the proper location. It is common for library books to be misplaced in a busy library).

- **Commandment 9.** Thou shalt remind library users not to reshelve their own materials (one of the main reasons books are misplaced).

- **Commandment 10.** Thou shalt pass a shelving test before shelving any books! (Lifesaver Tool 71.1. Shelving Test Handout)

 According to the code for the handicapped pertaining to wheelchair-bound library users, you should keep the height of your book shelves to four feet or less. For more information about barrier-free libraries, go to http://alexia.lis.uiuc.edu/~lis405/special/access/htm.

Pamela Bacon

# SHELVING TEST

NAME: _____   DATE: _____

1.  How are fiction books arranged on the shelf?_____
    _____

2.  How are nonfiction books arranged on the shelf? _____
    _____

3.  Where are SC books found? _____
    _____

4.  Where are E books found? _____
    _____

5.  Where are biographies shelved in the media center? _____
    _____

6.  Define the following library terms:
    to read a shelf: _____
    to shelve a book: _____
    to weed a book: _____

7.  Put the following fiction books in order:

    | Fiction<br>ABO | Fiction<br>DEE | Fiction<br>DAV | Fiction<br>CRA | Fiction<br>DON | Fiction<br>DIS |
    |---|---|---|---|---|---|
    | _____ | _____ | _____ | _____ | _____ | _____ |

8.  Put the following nonfiction books in order:

    | 300<br>ABO | 300<br>ABA | 300.10<br>ABO | 300.1<br>ABO | 300.01<br>ABA | 299<br>ABA |
    |---|---|---|---|---|---|
    | _____ | _____ | _____ | _____ | _____ | _____ |

9.  If two nonfiction call numbers have the same numbers, how do
    you know which one to shelve first (in order)? _____
    _____

10. Draw a simple line drawing of our media center layout showing
    the location of all book collections, periodicals, and other sections
    you feel are important.

**Lifesaver Tool 71.1.   Shelving Test Handout**

From *100 Library Lifesavers*. © 1999 Libraries Unlimited. (800) 237-6124.

# BOOK A NIGHT AT THE LIBRARY!

If you've never before been involved with student publishing, this is the place to start! The activity could be done at the elementary, middle, or senior high level. It's a great way to showcase young writers who are definitely worth checking out! (Lifesaver Tool 72.1. Invitation to Writers' Extravaganza)

## Lifesaver Tips

- Before beginning this project, solicit an agreement to participate from the public librarians. If hosting the event at the public library is not an option, the event could be hosted in the school cafeteria or auditorium. However, the connection with the public library is ideal.

- Tell students at the beginning of the year that a fine arts display night will be held at the public library.

- As the year goes by, remind students to set aside some of their best writing to display.

- Because this project involves unlimited possibilities for teaming with teachers, meet early and often to plan and organize the event.

- If you wish, combine forces with the art teacher to showcase both writing and art.

- Work closely with public librarians to choose a mutually acceptable date for the event.

- Obtain R.S.V.P.s and anticipate the number of guests expected. Coordination and communication with the public library staff at this point is critical.

- Work together to decorate for the big night. You might want to select a decorating theme (e.g., Dr. Seuss, Spring Fling, or a local tie-in could work well).

- Send out letters to parents early enough for parents to make arrangements, but not so early that they forget! Timing is critical.

- Send home frequent reminders of the event in your library newsletter.

- Continue to work with teachers to set aside library time and class time for work on book projects.

- Although participation in this event is optional, students should be encouraged to participate.

- Before the big night, discuss proper dress and etiquette with students.

- Send each member of the local press a personal, handwritten invitation.

- Take lots of pictures during the activity.

- After the event, process students' books and allow guests to check them out (with students' permission, of course).

 Address the public! Bookmark the public library site on your school library computers and e-mail with relevant notices and information.

Pamela Bacon

# INVITATION TO WRITERS' EXTRAVAGANZA

Date: _____

Dear Parents:

    You are cordially invited to attend our Writers' Extravaganza to be held at _____ o'clock at the Public Library. The Public Library is located at _____.

    Because viewing of books will take place all evening, you are welcome to come and go at any time between _____ and _____ o'clock. We are very proud to have hundreds of students' books to showcase this year. A variety of activities are scheduled throughout the evening, and refreshments will be available to make your viewing more pleasurable. If you have questions regarding this year's Extravaganza, please contact me.

          Sincerely,


          _____
          Media Specialist

..............................................................................................

R.S.V.P.
_____ I will be attending the Extravaganza.
        Number in party: _____
_____ I will not be attending the Extravaganza.
_____ I would like to donate refreshments.
_____ I wish to volunteer during the evening event.

Name: _____ Phone: _____

Address: _____

Best time to contact: _____

Parent of: _____

Comments: _____

_____

_____

Thank you for your feedback and support!

**Lifesaver Tool 72.1.**   **Invitation to Writers' Extravaganza**

# DISCIPLINE DOs AND DON'Ts

Like it or not, discipline is a big part of our job. And discipline in the media center is somewhat unique. Because we don't have the students in a homeroom, it can be hard to follow through. Certainly, support of the classroom teacher and principal is essential. The positive side, which works in our favor at the secondary level, is that visiting the media center is a privilege that can be taken away. At the elementary level, though, removing a child from the media center is not an option. No matter what level you teach, though, certain DOs and DON'Ts of discipline are universal. By the way, *do* take the discipline quiz and *don't* forget! (Lifesaver Tool 73.1. Discipline Decisions Quiz)

**DISCIPLINE DOs:**

- Follow through

- Follow the "F" rules—be fair, be flexible, make few rules

- Follow school guidelines

- Post rules clearly

- Praise good behavior

- Maintain good relationships with students

- Remember fair is not always equal

- Keep expectations high

- Make actions consistent

- Discipline when you are calm

## DISCIPLINE DON'Ts:

- Let students make you angry

- Yell or raise your voice

- Be inconsistent

- Play favorites

- Hold a grudge

- Forget to follow through

- Wait too long to discipline

- Make a decision when you're angry

- Be sarcastic

- Post rules you won't enforce

 Practice a little discipline yourself by enrolling in one of Lee Canter's independent study courses (1-800-669-9011). Earn three graduate credit hours from the comfort of your own home—if you're disciplined enough, that is!

Pamela Bacon

# DISCIPLINE DECISIONS

1.  Do you have rules clearly posted?                         Y      N

2.  Do you make your expectations known?                      Y      N

3.  Do you follow school discipline guidelines?               Y      N

4.  Do you control your anger when disciplining?              Y      N

5.  Do you have high expectations?                            Y      N

6.  Do you revise rules when needed?                          Y      N

7.  Do you know that fair is not always?                      Y      N

8.  Do you praise students often?                             Y      N

9.  Are you positive with students?                           Y      N

10. Are you flexible and fair with students?                  Y      N

11. Do you avoid yelling at students?                         Y      N

12. Are you comfortable with discipline?                      Y      N

13. Do you avoid holding grudges?                             Y      N

14. Do you regularly discipline students away from friends?   Y      N

15. Do you avoid sarcasm?                                     Y      N

*Note*: By now you have no doubt figured out that the correct response to each question is "Yes." If you answered "No" to any of the above questions, you know in which area(s) you need to concentrate.

**Lifesaver Tool 73.1.   Discipline Decisions Quiz**

From *100 Library Lifesavers*. © 1999 Libraries Unlimited (800) 237-6124.

# ARE YOU A FAKE?

The definition of this lifesaver is *fun*! Students learn to use the dictionary and understand the meaning of teamwork at the same time.

## Lifesaver Tips

- Choose five or six students to form a group panel.

- Shuffle word cards and choose one.

- Write the chosen word on the board.

- After the word is written, the panel meets privately to decide who should be the mystery panelist for the round.

- All the panelists look up the correct meaning of the word in the dictionary, but only the mystery panelist writes down the real definition.

- The other five panelists pretend to write down the definition, but really write down a fake definition.

- The librarian asks the students to read their definitions aloud.

- After reading the definitions, the librarian asks the students to vote for the definition they think is correct.

- After the voting, the mystery panelist stands and again reads the correct definition to the class.

- Change panels each library class.

 Dictionary dilemma? Keep a set of un-processed paperback dictionaries handy to use just for class activities.

Pamela Bacon

# Are You a Fake?

**Library Words:**

1. Reference
2. Periodical
3. Decimal
4. Cataloging
5. Carding
6. Shelving
7. Circulating
8. Reserve
9. Index
10. Research

**Book-Related Words:**

1. Spine
2. Plot
3. Illustration
4. Preface
5. Contents
6. Bibliography
7. Cover
8. Chapter
9. Dedication
10. Page

*Note*: Because many of these words have alternate meanings, be sure to advise students of the category before beginning the game!

**Lifesaver Tool 74.1.   Are You a Fake?**

# A SHARP IDEA!

I stumbled onto this lifesaver totally by accident. My teaching license was getting ready to expire (talk about procrastination!), so I immediately signed up for the next available workshop through the Bureau of Education and Research (BER). The workshop I attended just happened to be a workshop on children's literature presented by Dr. Peggy Sharp. What a lucky break—she is really one sharp lady (pardon the pun)! (Lifesaver Tool 75.1. Dr. Peggy Sharp's Internet Literature Sources)

## Lifesaver Tips

- Subscribe to *New Book News*, a newsletter devoted to the latest and best in children's literature, along with tips for application with students. For $15.95, you receive four issues cram-packed with ideas for K–6 teachers and librarians.

- Attend Sharp's annual workshop, "What's New in Children's Literature." Like her newsletter, this one-day workshop highlights the best new children's books. Not only do you receive wonderful ideas and lists of great new books, you can earn one graduate credit hour for attending. What a deal!

- Sharp's workshop, "The Library Media Specialist and the Teacher as Partners in Teaching the Research Process," is a wonderful resource filled with strategies on how to help students become better researchers.

- In addition to the above workshops, Sharp offers personalized workshops, developed especially for your school and students, that focus on books in your own library collection.

- For more information, contact Sharp directly at her Web site: www.peggysharp.com.

- You can also contact her by snail mail at the following address:

    P.O. Box 29078
    Portland, OR 97296

 After completing workshops or courses, post your certificate in your office. Everyone needs an "I Love Me!" wall.

Pamela Bacon

# A SHARP LIST:
# LITERATURE SOURCES ON THE NET

1.  **http://majordomo@lists.mindspring.com**—listserv for writers and illustrators of children's books.

2.  **http://kidsbooks-request@armory.com**—listserv for reviews of children's books.

3.  **http://majordomo@mail.rutgers.edu**—a professional exchange on children's books, authors, and research information.

4.  **http://listserv@psuvm.psu.edu**—a writers workshop that encourages writers to submit work and to engage in book discussions.

5.  **http://www.jps.net/gmreed/lit/authors.htm**—a Web site full of links to authors' links; it's the first place to go to find information about an author.

6.  **http://www.carolhurst.com/titles/gradetitles.html**—the Web site to read book reviews by grade level, author, title, or genre.

7.  **http://www.scholastic.com/**—one of the very best literature-based sites on the Internet just for kids. Find links to Scholastic's most popular books: *The Babysitter's Club, The Magic School Bus, Animorphs,* and more.

8.  **http://www.parentsplace.com/readroom/index.html**—a Web site full of thousands of best books for kids.

**Lifesaver Tool 75.1.   Dr. Peggy Sharp's Internet Literature Sources**

# IMPROVE YOUR CITE!

Is it any wonder, with all the new technology and sources available these days, that students have a hard time knowing how to cite sources for a bibliography page? Distribute Lifesaver Tool 76.1 (Sample Internet Reference Cards) to students while they do computer researching; these cards will help them find all the information they need! Their cites will definitely improve!

## Lifesaver Tips

### BASIC FORMAT FOR SOURCES

- Author's last name, Author's first name. "Title of Document." Title of Complete Work (if applicable). Version or File Number, if applicable. Document date or date of last revision (if different from access date). Protocol and address, access path, or directories (date of access).

- FTP (File Transfer Protocol). *Example*: Bruckman, Amy. "Approaches to Managing Deviant Behavior in Virtual Communities." April 1994. ftp://ftp.media.mit.edu/pub/asb/papers.

- WWW (World Wide Web). *Example*: Burka, Lauren P. "A Hypertext History of Multi-User Dimensions." The MUDdex. 1993. http://www.apocalypse.org/pub/u/lpb/muddex/essay/ (December 5, 1994).

- E-Mail, Listserv, and Newsgroup. *Examples*: Bruckman, Amy S. "MOOSE Crossing Proposal. mediamoo@media.mit.edu (December 20, 1994). Seabrook, Richard H. C. "Community and Progress." cybermind@jefferson.village.virginia.edu (January 22, 1994). Thomson, Barry. "Virtual Reality." Personal e-mail (January 25, 1995).

- CD-ROM. *Example*: Zieger, Herman E. "Aldehyde." The Software Toolworks Multimedia Encyclopedia. Version 1.5. Software Toolworks. Boston: Grolier, 1992.

- Source of Information: Walker, Janice R. "Columbia Online Style." Internet. http://www.cas.ust.edu/engligh/walker/mla.html/ (May 11, 1998).

 E-mail an LM_NET buddy from a faraway state! Share interesting cultural information with students!

Pamela Bacon

# INTERNET REFERENCE CARD

| # _____ | **INTERNET REFERENCE CARD** |

SOURCE: _____

HTTP ADDRESS: _____

_____

DATE OF SOURCE:_____

DATE OF SEARCHING: _____

AUTHOR'S LAST NAME: _____

AUTHOR'S FIRST NAME: _____

SOURCE TITLE: _____

_____

VERSION/FILE NUMBER: _____

<br>

| # _____ | **INTERNET REFERENCE CARD** |

SOURCE: _____

HTTP ADDRESS: _____

_____

DATE OF SOURCE:_____

DATE OF SEARCHING: _____

AUTHOR'S LAST NAME: _____

AUTHOR'S FIRST NAME: _____

SOURCE TITLE: _____

_____

VERSION/FILE NUMBER: _____

**Lifesaver Tool 76.1. Sample Internet Reference Cards**

# READING IS A MYSTERY

The fun thing about the mystery reader idea is that the reader can be anyone. Kids are just excited to have someone new read to them once in a while. Any person willing to come and share a story will work—it's best, however, if the time they come in is not a mystery to *you*!

## Lifesaver Tips

- Allow mystery readers to choose their own books. Chances are, they have a favorite from their own childhood they'd like to share.

- Set up mystery readers' dates in advance—but not so far in advance that they forget!

- Keep a calendar of mystery readers' dates.

- Keep a backup reader or lesson handy in case of a no-show!

- Take pictures of the mystery readers reading to the kids. Post the pictures on a bulletin board, in your newsletter, or, even better, in the local paper!

- Keep in mind that any reader can be a mystery reader. Our school's custodian was one of the best mystery readers I've used. And it's nice for students to see that person in a different role!

- Principals are an obvious choice for a mystery reader—and they're always fun for the kids!

- People in costume make excellent mystery readers—especially those dressed as characters from their books!

- Always send a thank-you note to the mystery reader; he or she has donated precious time!

- If you're a concrete sequential person (like me!), set up mystery readers for each month at the beginning of the school year. Then, when the time gets close, send a postcard reminding the mystery reader of the date! (Lifesaver Tool 77.1. Mystery Reader Reminder Form)

- Offer students clues, the week before, to the identity of the mystery reader—it will build suspense!

- Keep in mind that children from other classes can be wonderful mystery readers!

 High school students make excellent mystery readers for elementary and middle school grades! It's no mystery that kids listen better for other kids!

Pamela Bacon

# MYSTERY READER REMINDER CARD

To: _____

    Greetings! Thank you for agreeing to be a mystery reader on _____ (date) at _____ o'clock. I am very much looking forward to your visit. Please call me at _____ if you have any questions or need a good read-aloud title. Have a great day!

    Sincerely,


_____

Media Specialist

**Lifesaver Tool 77.1.   Mystery Reader Reminder Form**

# FRIENDS OF THE LIBRARY

I have not yet formed my Friends of the Library group, but I am excited about doing so in the future. (Lifesaver Tool 78.1. Friends of the Library Invitation Letter) Therefore, I decided to ask some practicing colleagues to share their success stories with library support groups. Here they are!

## Lifesaver Tips

- An excellent reference is the *Friends of the Libraries Sourcebook* by Sandy Dolnick. She targets many types of Friends groups, as well as school library groups. Visit the ALA's (American Library Association) home page for more information, http://www.ala.org/.

- E-mail ALA. This support group responds to inquiries in just a day or two.

- Contact your local PTO group. These involved parents can be a wonderful resource.

- Become the head or chair of the group if no one else volunteers!

 Don't overlook your principal as one of your most important "friends"!

Pamela Bacon

# INVITATION TO JOIN
# FRIENDS OF THE LIBRARY

Date: _____

Dear _____:

This letter is to inquire whether you would be interested in joining our Friends of the Library group. Our support group meets on a monthly basis in the school media center to discuss issues concerning our library. The meetings are informal, and, for your comfort, coffee and donuts are provided.

Our next Friends Club meeting is

_____.

If you would like more information about our group, please contact me or, better yet, come to our next meeting. We hope to see you there!

Sincerely,


Media Specialist

**Lifesaver Tool 78.1.** **Friends of the Library Invitation Letter**

# YOU'RE QUITE A CHARACTER!

My good friend Nancy came up with the idea of having a Character Day to celebrate National Book Week. (Lifesaver Tool 79.1. Book Characters Sign-Up Sheet) It's no surprise to me, or to any of the teachers with whom Nancy works, that it was a huge success! Nancy is much like Rapunzel—anything she has a hand in turns to solid gold!

## Lifesaver Tips

- Start planning months in advance for this project to be successful. Allow those teachers (and administrators!) who hate to dress up to choose an "easy" character. One teacher at Nancy's school, for example, who didn't want to participate did finally agree to dress as *The Boy in the Red Jacket*. (Surprise—he simply wore a red jacket and a sign telling who he was!) As simple as his costume was, the kids got a kick out of seeing this naysayer participate in the fun-filled activity.

- Remember, you set the tone for the entire week. Be sure to choose a truly outrageous costume and let your enthusiasm be contagious.

- Tell teachers to give a clue each day as to the identity of their books' characters. On Friday (or the last day of the program), the dress-up will occur.

- Plan a convocation for teachers in costume to parade past the students. This program can be very simple or very detailed—depending on how much time you want to spend. One teacher, for example, had teachers read excerpts from the books containing the characters they were promoting. Another teacher simply had teachers parade in and out of classrooms and allowed students to guess the mystery characters' identities.

- Offer to help teachers in choosing a character or in making up hints.

- Ask teachers who still won't participate to sit with the kids during the program and monitor behavior. We don't want the kids being real "characters" with no supervision!

 Offer a wide variety of suggestions to your staff—including *easy* characters such as *Farmer Boy* by Laura Ingalls Wilder or *The Kid in the Red Jacket* by Barbara Park.

Nancy Witty, Media Specialist,
Rockville Elementary School, Rockville, IN

# BOOK CHARACTERS SIGN-UP SHEET!

| Teacher | Character | Book Title | Need Help? |
|---------|-----------|------------|------------|
| | | | |
| | | | |
| | | | |
| | | | |
| | | | |
| | | | |
| | | | |
| | | | |
| | | | |
| | | | |
| | | | |
| | | | |
| | | | |
| | | | |
| | | | |
| | | | |
| | | | |
| | | | |
| | | | |
| | | | |
| | | | |
| | | | |
| | | | |
| | | | |
| | | | |
| | | | |

**Lifesaver Tool 79.1.** Book Characters Sign-Up Sheet

# YOU'RE ON DISPLAY!

This lifesaver is another way to connect with teachers in a fun, positive way. Kids love to try to guess the identity of the teacher of the week, and it's a great way to fill up your display case all year!

## Lifesaver Tips

- Send a letter to teachers at the beginning of each year asking them to participate. (Lifesaver Tool 80.1. Mystery Teacher Sign-Up Letter)

- Every week a different teacher is highlighted in the display case. The mystery teacher of the week brings in childhood pictures, favorite books, hobby clues, and any other items of interest that express his or her personality.

- The items should tell something about the teacher, yet not make it too easy for students to guess the identity.

- During library class or study hall, students guess who they believe is the mystery teacher. The first student to be drawn out with the correct teacher named wins a prize.

- A suggestion for a prize is lunch with that special teacher!

- Back the display case with a bright fabric and post a laminated "Who am I?" inside the case. Fill the case each week (or month) with items from a different teacher.

- On Friday, ask the principal to announce the identity of the mystery teacher and the winning student!

- Have plenty of guess cards ready. (Lifesaver Tool 80.2. Sample Mystery Teacher Guess Cards)

 Limit your staff to specific categories; by the end of the school year some teachers will bring in everything but the kitchen sink!

Nancy Witty, Media Specialist,
Rockville Elementary School, Rockville, IN

# MYSTERY TEACHER SIGN-UP LETTER

Dear Teachers:

Once again it is time to sign up to be a Mystery Teacher of the Week! As in past years, each week the "Who am I?" display case will be filled with personality clues. The students will attempt to guess the mystery teacher's identity and one lucky student will win a prize. If you have participated in the past, great! Just try to provide different clues this time. Remember, one of the most interesting clues is your favorite childhood book. If you don't have a copy, let me know and I'll try to find a copy for you. Other items include:

baby/childhood pictures

hobby or craft

pictures of a pet (or children!)

favorite childhood book(s)

any other items which describe *you*!

If you would like to participate this year, please fill out the bottom of this letter and return to me by _____.

Thanks for your help—this idea wouldn't work without *you*!

Sincerely,

_____

Media Specialist

...............................................................................................................................

Teacher: _____

_____ Yes, I'll be a teacher of the week!
_____ I would like my week to be one of the following:

Choice 1: _____

Choice 2: _____

Choice 3: _____

_____ Maybe next year!
_____ Comments:

**Lifesaver Tool 80.1. Mystery Teacher Sign-Up Letter**

# SAMPLE MYSTERY TEACHER GUESS CARDS

WHO AM I?

Who do you think is this week's mystery teacher?

_____
(TEACHER'S NAME)

YOUR NAME: _____
GRADE: _____
DATE: _____

WHO AM I?

Who do you think is this week's mystery teacher?

_____
(TEACHER'S NAME)

YOUR NAME: _____
GRADE: _____
DATE: _____

WHO AM I?

Who do you think is this week's mystery teacher?

_____
(TEACHER'S NAME)

YOUR NAME: _____
GRADE: _____
DATE: _____

**Lifesaver Tool 80.2.** **Sample Mystery Teacher Guess Cards**

# TAKE THE WORK OUT OF TEAMWORK

There's no doubt about it—teaming with teachers can be hard work. But the following four steps can be taken to make the task a little easier. The first lifesaver, finding time, is often the most difficult on the ladder of teamwork success.

## Lifesaver Tips

**T    TIME**    Take TIME out of your busy schedule to work with teachers!

- Some schools provide a rough instructional schedule for teachers to fill in tentative unit dates. If your school doesn't already do this, suggest it to the principal. Having a rough time line of teachers' schedules is invaluable for planning purposes. (Lifesaver Tool 81.1. Subject Area Collaboration Handout)

- If your school doesn't have a schedule, look back over your teachers' sign-in schedule book from last year. You should be able to get a general idea of the subjects and when they are covered.

- To lure teachers into the library for planning interdisciplinary units, bribe them with donuts each month (before school usually works better than after school!).

- Purchasing subject-related materials is another enticing way to draw in teachers.

**E   EQUAL**   Make sure both you and the teacher have EQUAL parts in planning, implementing, and evaluating the lesson!

- Give and take in equal measure. Cooperation in teamwork is critical.
- When team teaching with one teacher, insist on grading half the projects (this shows teachers that you're serious and committed to teaming; the word soon gets around!).
- Brainstorm lesson ideas during teaming sessions and use suggestions from each team member.
- Team with all teachers—not just your favorites!

**A   ATTITUDE**   The better your ATTITUDE and flexibility, the more successful your project will be!

- Be familiar with the lesson before a teacher comes into the library.
- Be prepared to monitor and adjust the lesson as needed—with the teacher's permission, of course!
- Don't be put off by teachers who refuse to team with you—keep trying.
- Be positive (but firm) with teachers who try to use you as a drop-off service.

**M   MEET**   MEET with teachers before and after the lesson (plan before, evaluate after!).

- Use a follow-up form to solicit specific feedback.
- Meet regularly with teachers.
- Be familiar with teachers' textbooks and supplemental materials.
- Getting on book adoption committees can be a lifesaver!
- Volunteer (as time allows) for curriculum committees.
- Hang out in the teacher's lounge. Often we librarians tend to hibernate in our media centers, but spending time in the teacher's hub can end up being a time-saver as far as teaming goes!

Before trying out for the team, read *Helping Teachers Teach: A School Library Media Specialist's Role* by Philip Turner. This source is packed with helpful information on how to team effectively and collaborate with teachers. It's available through Libraries Unlimited (http://www.lu.com/) or 1-800-237-6124 for $26.50.

Pamela Bacon

# GO TEAM!

Subject Area Collaboration Checklist

Grade Level _____

|  | **Language** | **Math** | **History** | **Science** |
|---|---|---|---|---|
| August | _____ | _____ | _____ | _____ |
| September | _____ | _____ | _____ | _____ |
| October | _____ | _____ | _____ | _____ |
| November | _____ | _____ | _____ | _____ |
| December | _____ | _____ | _____ | _____ |
| January | _____ | _____ | _____ | _____ |
| February | _____ | _____ | _____ | _____ |
| March | _____ | _____ | _____ | _____ |
| April | _____ | _____ | _____ | _____ |
| May | _____ | _____ | _____ | _____ |
| June | _____ | _____ | _____ | _____ |

*Note*: Use the above lifesaver as a checklist to make teaming more intentional. Place a check under the appropriate subject when a teacher brings a class to the library. Keep copies of all handouts for lesson details.

**Lifesaver Tool 81.1. Subject Area Collaboration Handout**

# TWO CENTS' WORTH

The proverb "A Penny Saved Is a Penny Earned" is certainly true of this lifesaving fund-raiser. (Lifesaver Tool 82.1. Penny-Tracking Form) You'll be surprised by how quickly those pennies add up to wonderful new books for your media center!

## Lifesaver Tips

- You can ask students to donate silver, too, but I prefer just to focus on pennies. I've found many parents all too happy to get rid of copper coins, but sometimes not as willing to part with the silver!

- For an added incentive, keep track of how many pennies are brought in by each grade level. At the end of the year, offer a prize to the winning class (ice cream works well—paid for with pennies, of course!).

- Put a library recognition plate in books purchased with pennies, along with the year the book was purchased. Keep books in a special section.

- At the end of the year, calculate with the students how many pennies it will take to buy a book! Students learn the value of money and appreciate the rising price of books at the same time!

- Use the theme "Reading Is Worth Every Cent!"

 If all you've got to spend are pennies, save them up and purchase *When Your Library Budget Is Almost Zero* by Lesley Farmer. It's worth every penny!

Pamela Bacon

# PENNY-TRACKING FORM

Month: _____

| Grade | | Month Total | Grand Total |
|:---:|:---:|:---:|:---:|
| K | _____ | _____ | _____ |
| 1 | _____ | _____ | _____ |
| 2 | _____ | _____ | _____ |
| 3 | _____ | _____ | _____ |
| 4 | _____ | _____ | _____ |
| 5 | _____ | _____ | _____ |
| 6 | _____ | _____ | _____ |
| 7 | _____ | _____ | _____ |
| 8 | _____ | _____ | _____ |
| 9 | _____ | _____ | _____ |
| 10 | _____ | _____ | _____ |
| 11 | _____ | _____ | _____ |
| 12 | _____ | _____ | _____ |

## *Reading Is Worth Every Cent!*

**Lifesaver Tool 82.1.**  **Penny-Tracking Form**

# SHELF-SITTER

Shelf-sitters are caretakers for shelves. The shelf-sitter is similar to the Adopt-a-Highway program—the goal being to keep a section of road (in this case books) neat and tidy. Just as road users sometimes litter while driving down the road, library users sometimes litter the shelves by putting books in the wrong places. That's where shelf-sitters come in. Not only is this idea a lifesaver for you, it's also an excellent teaching tool for students to learn Dewey in a meaningful way.

## SHELF-SITTER STEPS TO ADOPT A SHELF!

A **ARRANGE** (straighten shelf)

D **DUST**

O **ORDER**

P **PUT BOOKS,** which are out of order, on cart

T **TURN IN** form (check off list!)

## Lifesaver Tips

- Before adopting this strategy, teach students Dewey basics, then teach them again. The last thing you want is a hardworking student diligently rearranging all the books on the shelf if they were already in order to begin with!

- Practice with students on just a small section of shelves before letting them loose on their own shelves.

- Give a pretest by messing up books on a shelf and then having students put them in order. (To save time, write down on note cards which books you moved and have other students test on the same shelf.)

- Rather than assigning shelves to an entire class, I've found it works best just to take volunteers who really want to help.

- Check shelves randomly for accuracy once the program starts.

- Obviously, every library shelf arrangement is different. For convenience, three Lifesaver Tool charts are included. The first one is for fiction, the second for nonfiction, and a third is included to list other shelves. (Lifesaver Tool 83.1. Shelf-Sitter Schedule: Fiction; Lifesaver Tool 83.2. Shelf-Sitter Schedule: Nonfiction; Lifesaver Tool 83.3. Shelf-Sitter Schedule: Other Category)

 Brighten up when it comes to shelving. The Library Store (1-800-548-7204) has a wonderful new three-shelf cart in a variety of colors. It's small, easy to store, and a fun change from tan and gray!

Pamela Bacon

# SHELF-SITTER SCHEDULE

| NAME | SHELF | DONE (X) | INITIALS-M.S. |
|---|---|---|---|
|  | FIC |  |  |
|  | FIC |  |  |
|  | FIC |  |  |
|  | FIC |  |  |
|  | FIC |  |  |
|  | FIC |  |  |
|  | FIC |  |  |
|  | FIC |  |  |
|  | FIC |  |  |
|  | FIC |  |  |
|  | FIC |  |  |
|  | FIC |  |  |
|  | FIC |  |  |
|  | FIC |  |  |
|  | FIC |  |  |
|  | FIC |  |  |
|  | FIC |  |  |
|  | FIC |  |  |
|  | FIC |  |  |
|  | FIC |  |  |
|  | FIC |  |  |
|  | FIC |  |  |
|  | FIC |  |  |
|  | FIC |  |  |
|  | FIC |  |  |

**Lifesaver Tool 83.1.   Shelf-Sitter Schedule: Fiction**

# SHELF-SITTER SCHEDULE

| NAME | SHELF | DONE (X) | INITIALS-M.S. |
|---|---|---|---|
| | NONFIC | | |
| | NONFIC | | |
| | NONFIC | | |
| | NONFIC | | |
| | NONFIC | | |
| | NONFIC | | |
| | NONFIC | | |
| | NONFIC | | |
| | NONFIC | | |
| | NONFIC | | |
| | NONFIC | | |
| | NONFIC | | |
| | NONFIC | | |
| | NONFIC | | |
| | NONFIC | | |
| | NONFIC | | |
| | NONFIC | | |
| | NONFIC | | |
| | NONFIC | | |
| | NONFIC | | |
| | NONFIC | | |
| | NONFIC | | |
| | NONFIC | | |
| | NONFIC | | |

**Lifesaver Tool 83.2.   Shelf-Sitter Schedule: Nonfiction**

# SHELF-SITTER SCHEDULE

| NAME | SHELF | DONE (X) | INITIALS-M.S. |
|------|-------|----------|---------------|
|  |  |  |  |
|  |  |  |  |
|  |  |  |  |
|  |  |  |  |
|  |  |  |  |
|  |  |  |  |
|  |  |  |  |
|  |  |  |  |
|  |  |  |  |
|  |  |  |  |
|  |  |  |  |
|  |  |  |  |
|  |  |  |  |
|  |  |  |  |
|  |  |  |  |
|  |  |  |  |
|  |  |  |  |
|  |  |  |  |
|  |  |  |  |
|  |  |  |  |
|  |  |  |  |
|  |  |  |  |
|  |  |  |  |
|  |  |  |  |
|  |  |  |  |
|  |  |  |  |
|  |  |  |  |

**Lifesaver Tool 83.3.**   **Shelf-Sitter Schedule: Other Category**

# V.I.P.
# (VERY IMPORTANT PERSON)

If you're looking for a thoughtful, yet inexpensive, way to show your appreciation to your faithful volunteer, this lifesaver could be a V.I.P. (Very Important Part!) of your library program! (Lifesaver Tool 84.1. Sample V.I.P. Award Certificate)

## Lifesaver Tips

- A variety of generic certificates are available for purchase through DEMCO (1-800-356-1200), Paper Direct (1-800-272-7377), or at variety stores and office supply stores.

- Personally, I prefer crafting my own personalized certificates with the PrintMaster Gold software program.

- Along with the certificates, write a letter of appreciation to be signed by both the media specialist and your building principal.

- Ask your building principal to add a personal note of appreciation to the bottom of the letter for added thoughtfulness.

- At the end of the year, present each parent who volunteered with a framed certificate and letter of appreciation.

- Thank-you notes written and illustrated by students are also an excellent way to show appreciation to your V.I.P.!

- Try to find a unique, inexpensive gift to add to your V.I.P.'s care package. An inspirational bookmark is a perfect way to remind your volunteer to take time to read over the summer.

- Browse used bookstores for treasured books to give volunteers.

 Don't overlook AARP (American Association of Retired People) as an excellent source for qualified helpers. They won't be the only seniors in the school!

Pamela Bacon

## V.I.P. Award Certificate

*VIP AWARD*

## for outstanding effort and support in the library

Principal

Media Specialist

**Lifesaver Tool 84.1.** **Sample V.I.P. Award Certificate**

# READERS ARE LEADERS

All too often, students are afraid to admit that they enjoy reading. Not wanting to be labeled bookworms by peers, especially in junior high, many avid readers won't admit they love to read. The solution I came up with is to make being a reader more desirable. My desire to turn attitudes and pages was the inspiration for this lifesaver. (Lifesaver Tool 85.1. Readers Are Leaders Application Form)

## Lifesaver Tips

- Attempt to persuade popular students to jump on board so that others will follow. Turn peer pressure into a positive thing.

- For manageability, limit the number in the Readers Are Leaders group.

- The Readers Are Leaders group functions independently of the school's reading club; any student is eligible. This select group of students are reading role models for other students.

- Readers Are Leaders members should enjoy certain privileges of membership. Examples might include: library helper membership, library passes, public library trips, book club officers, Friends of the Library club membership, free books, etc.

- Interested students must apply and be accepted.

- Form a selection committee to assist with the difficult task of choosing new members.

- Use book fair funds to purchase exclusive sweatshirts for members.

- Readers Are Leaders should be instrumental in planning and setting up book fairs.

- Use book fair funds to host school dances.

- Use book fair funds to host author visits to the school.

- Publicize your Readers Are Leaders group both in the school and in the community.

 DEMCO's "READ" shirts will fit your students to a "T"! The colorful shirts are available in sizes for both children and adults and are reasonably priced (1-800-356-1200).

Pamela Bacon

# READERS ARE LEADERS
# APPLICATION

Name: _____  Date: _____

Address: _____

_____

Phone: _____ Parent's name(s): _____

Grade: _____ Date of birth: _____

G.P.A.: _____Hobbies: _____

Club memberships (including sports): _____

_____

Please type answers to the following questions. Submit this application, your typed answers, and a letter of nomination by_____.

Thank you.

1. What is the last book you have read? _____
_____

2. Who is your favorite author? _____

3. How much time (per week) do you spend reading? _____

4. What types of books do you most enjoy reading? _____

5. What is the worst book you have ever read? Please give a reason for your opinion. _____
_____

6. Do you enjoy writing? (poems, stories, plays, songs, etc.)_____

7. If you are selected, do you have enough time to donate to the book club as an officer? _____

8. What are your current and future after-school obligations? _____
_____

9. Do you regularly visit the public library? Why/why not?_____
_____

10. What is your current English/reading/language arts grade?_____

**Lifesaver Tool 85.1.  Readers Are Leaders Application Form**

# JUST THE FAX, MA'AM!

If you just want the "fax," you'll need a fax cover sheet. After a trip to the copier, you have all the forms you need to get the job done! (Lifesaver Tool 86.1. Sample Fax Cover Sheet)

## Lifesaver Tips

- Keep all your original forms in your file cabinet.

- Keep copies of forms in marked manila file folders.

- Assign a student helper the job of monitoring the form files so that you don't run out.

- Always save copies of outgoing faxes. You never know when you might need to verify an order or show confirmation that a fax was sent.

- Keep an Outgoing Faxes file with all faxes sent. Label with the year.

- To fax fast, type in your school's fax number (and other information that never changes) and photocopy a good supply to keep next to your fax machine.

- Adding clip art is another good way to personalize your fax cover sheet.

 Golfers aren't the only ones who need a caddy! Check out the Classroom Caddy from The Library Store (1-800-548-7204). It's par for the course when it comes to organization!

Pamela Bacon

# FROM THE MEDIA CENTER

Fax Number: _____

Date: _____ Time: _____

To:         _____

            _____

From:       _____

            _____

Comments: _____

_____

_____

_____

Number of pages sent: _____ (excluding cover)

Reply Requested:      Yes       No

For questions regarding fax,

    please call _____ or fax _____.

From *100 Library Lifesavers.* © 1999 Libraries Unlimited. (800) 237-6124.

**Lifesaver Tool 86.1.   Sample Fax Cover Sheet**

# WHAT'S YOUR SIGN?

This lifesaver takes the media center one step further by asking each student the purpose of his or her visits. Therefore, when students sign in to study, they can be held just a little more accountable! I hope you'll see signs of better time on task with this lifesaver. (Lifesaver Tool 87.1. Media Center Log Sheet)

## Lifesaver Tips

- Ask all students to sign in and out of the library—even if they leave to use the rest room. If they have to sign in and out, they may ask to leave less often!

- Because this form makes it so much easier to keep track of students, tell them to sign up or ship out!

- If a student consistently forgets to sign in, just sign him or her out for a day or two to jog the student's memory!

 To save time and trouble, purchase the Stay Put Pen from The Library Store (1-800-548-7204). There's no guarantee your students will stay put, but at least your pen will!

Pamela Bacon

# MEDIA CENTER SIGN-IN/OUT

DATE: _____

| PERIOD | NAME | PURPOSE OF VISIT | TIME IN | TIME OUT |
|--------|------|------------------|---------|----------|
|  |  |  |  |  |
|  |  |  |  |  |
|  |  |  |  |  |
|  |  |  |  |  |
|  |  |  |  |  |
|  |  |  |  |  |
|  |  |  |  |  |
|  |  |  |  |  |
|  |  |  |  |  |
|  |  |  |  |  |
|  |  |  |  |  |
|  |  |  |  |  |
|  |  |  |  |  |
|  |  |  |  |  |
|  |  |  |  |  |
|  |  |  |  |  |
|  |  |  |  |  |
|  |  |  |  |  |
|  |  |  |  |  |
|  |  |  |  |  |

S = STUDY      R = RESEARCH      F = FREE READING      T = TEST      C = COMPUTER
DL = DISTANCE LEARNING      * * OTHERS, PLEASE LIST ABOVE!

**Lifesaver Tool 87.1.   Media Center Log Sheet**

From *100 Library Lifesavers*. © 1999 Libraries Unlimited. (800) 237-6124.

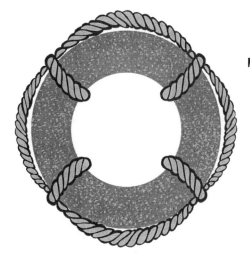

# TEACHER'S CHOICE: RATING AND ROUTING FORM

This lifesaver does double duty. It's a quick, easy way to get teachers' feedback on videotapes and it's a routing form, too. (Lifesaver Tool 88.1. Rating and Routing Form)

## Lifesaver Tips

- On a standard copier, reduce Lifesaver Tool 88.1 to four lifesavers to fit on a page (size should be small enough to be taped on the front of the videotape!).

- Run off multiple routing forms on a sheet of colored paper. Ask a student helper to cut forms apart and let you know when the supply is getting short.

- Keep copies of routing forms for reference. When weeding, it might be helpful to know, for example, that two teachers rated the video four stars. On the other hand, if the video received a low rating by all teachers, you may want to consider ordering a different video on the same subject.

- Let teachers know where used routing forms are kept. When they are choosing a video to show, they may want to learn other teachers' opinions about the video, especially if the videos travel between different schools.

- Keep a copy of the routing form when a video leaves to let you know it is in circulation. If the video does not return, at least you know where to start looking!

 Purchase a video maintenance kit from The Library Store (1-800-548-7204). At $18.95, it's still much cheaper than buying new videotapes!

Pamela Bacon

# TEACHER'S CHOICE: RATING AND ROUTING FORM

Title: _____ Date Purchased: _____

Teacher 1: _____

Rating: _____ Comments: _____

Teacher 2: _____

Rating: _____ Comments: _____

Teacher 3: _____

Rating: _____ Comments: _____

Teacher 4: _____

Rating: _____ Comments: _____

Teacher 5: _____

Rating: _____ Comments: _____

* = Poor   ** = Fair   *** = Good   **** = Excellent

**Lifesaver Tool 88.1.**   **Rating and Routing Form**

# MAGIC MARKERS

No ordinary shelf markers, these "magic markers" are personalized to mark a spot on shelves for individual students. Students have their own markers so that they can quickly and easily reshelve their books the following week. (Lifesaver Tool 89.1. Sample Shelf Marker) You can't color with these magic markers, but they do add color to your media center!

## Lifesaver Tips

- Instead of paying for expensive ready-made shelf markers, ask local businesses to donate plastic.

- Allow students to decorate their own shelf markers to illustrate their unique personalities.

- Remind students that they may want to include titles or pictures of their favorite books.

- If shelf markers fall out, place them in a basket to distribute during the next library time.

- Avid readers may have several shelf markers.

- If possible, obtain plastic pieces in bright colors to liven up the shelves.

- If plastic is unattainable, cardboard can be used instead.

- Keep markers in the library, rather than in the classroom, for easy use.

 Use paint stirrers from your local hardware store for shelf markers. If you're feeling ambitious, spray paint them in your school colors!

Toni Buzzeo, Library Media Specialist,
Longfellow School, Portland, ME

# MAGIC MARKER

ILLUSTRATION/
DECORATION >

I
LOVE
BOOKS!

READ!!!

MANDY M.

5S

< PLASTIC OR
CARDBOARD

WRITE ON BOTH
SIDES       >

< NAME

< TEACHER

**EXAMPLE OF STUDENT MAGIC MARKER**

**Lifesaver Tool 89.1.   Sample Shelf Marker**

# WE'VE GOT YOU COVERED!

Making new covers for old books is one way to boost circulation of often-overlooked classics. (Lifesaver Tool 90.1. Covering Books) Unfortunately, students do judge books by their covers!

## Lifesaver Tips

- Only use completed, well-crafted covers on library books.

- Use only student-made covers that bring out the book's best qualities.

- Covers should give a hint to what the book is about.

- Covers should include illustration, title, author, illustrator, publisher, inside blurb, information about the author, and awards or reviews the book has received.

- Front flap should include a blurb (what the book is about).

- Information about the author appears on back flap.

- Front and back covers should be illustrated.

- Hold a contest to encourage students to enter high-quality book covers.

- Make this activity a library lesson. Students who wish to finish the covers may submit them to the library for consideration!

 Take photos of students who submitted great covers and send them to your local newspaper! It's a snap!

Pamela Bacon

# IT'S A COVER-UP

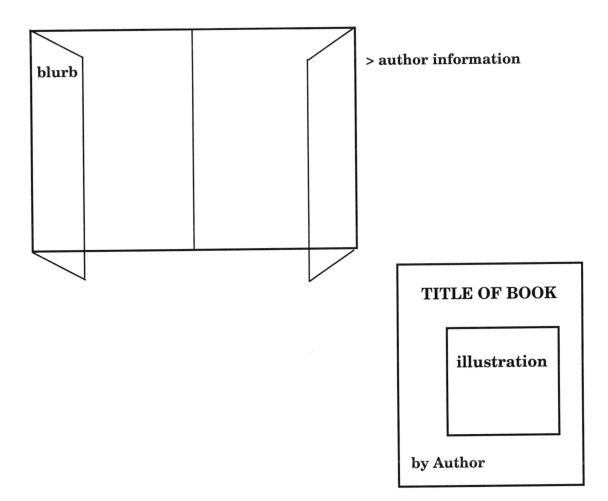

blurb

> author information

TITLE OF BOOK

illustration

by Author

**Lifesaver Tool 90.1.    Covering Books**

# BIG WHEELS KEEP ON READING

If you're looking for a hands-on activity to reinforce literary concepts, look no further. Character wheels are a great way to review books and dictionary skills. (Lifesaver Tool 91.1. The Character Wheel Bookplate) These are not your average bookplates!

## Lifesaver Tips

- Distribute a paper plate to each student.

- Students should begin by drawing a circle in the middle of each plate.

- The circle should be large enough to include the title, the author, and the main character of their assigned book.

- Students should then draw the five "spokes" of the wheel.

- On each spoke, the student should record a character trait about the main character. For example, Anne Frank's five traits (*A Diary of a Young Girl*) could be playful, creative, thoughtful, intuitive, and determined.

- At least three of the five words should be new vocabulary words.

- Give a dictionary and/or a thesaurus to each student.

- Review with the group how to use each reference tool.

- Assist students with finding the best words to describe their characters.

- Students should write down the meanings of new words on note cards.

- When students have filled in the character wheel, they should add color.

- Hang completed wheels from the ceiling with fishing line after each student presents his or her bookplate to the class.

 A clothespin attached to the end of a fishing line works great for hanging items from the ceiling. You won't catch a fish, but you're bound to have an eye-catching display.

Pamela Bacon

# CHARACTERS ON WHEELS

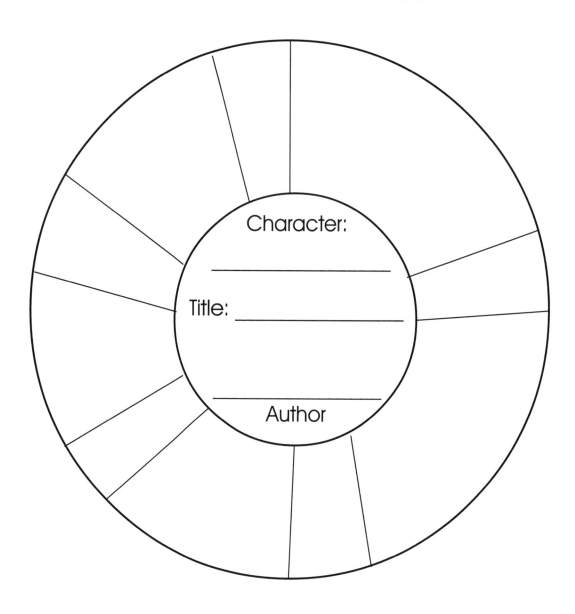

**Lifesaver Tool 91.1.   The Character Wheel Bookplate**

# LM_NET: IF YOU CAN'T BEAT 'EM, JOIN 'EM!

Because this listserv is unbeatable for ideas, resources, and support from practicing professionals in the field of library science, my best advice is to join right away!

## Lifesaver Tips

- After joining, be prepared to receive a lot of e-mail.

- Go through mail daily. If you don't, it really piles up!

- This listserv is not designed for public librarians—rather, it serves to meet the growing needs solely of school librarians.

- For best results, thoroughly read the information immediately forwarded to you upon signing on. The etiquette tips are especially helpful for new e-mail users.

- Check out the FAQ (Frequently Asked Questions) section to avoid asking a question another member recently asked the group.

- If you're new to the group, search through the archives for helpful back issues full of great ideas.

- LM_NET also has links to other interesting professional sites.

- The LM_NET member directory is now under construction. This tool should prove a wonderful resource and method to network with our colleagues from afar.

- Lifesaver Tool 92.1 (How to Join LM_NET) tells you all you need to know to become a member (computer and Internet access not included!).

 If you're going on vacation, use LM_NET's NO MAIL option. Just don't forget to change the settings when you get back—you'd hate to miss even a single message!

Pamela Bacon

# EIGHT GREAT STEPS TO LM_NET

1. Sign up for local Internet access.

2. Obtain an e-mail address.

3. Become familiar and comfortable with e-mail.

4. Send an e-mail message (using all capital letters) to LISTSERV@LISTSERV.SYR.EDU.

5. In the first line of the message type: SUBSCRIBE LM_NET Firstname Lastname (do not use a comma or quotes and be sure to put your name in the correct space, e.g., SUBSCRIBE LM_NET Pamela Bacon).

6. The LM_NET listserv computer will respond with an informative, lengthy message asking for confirmation. If you follow directions properly, your name will be added to the group!

7. If you have problems signing on to the group, contact: pmilbury@ericir.syr.edu.

8. The Web address for LM_NET is: http://ericir.edu/lm_net/.

### *GOOD LUCK AND WELCOME ABOARD!*

**Lifesaver Tool 92.1.   How to Join LM_NET**

From *100 Library Lifesavers.* © 1999 Libraries Unlimited. (800) 237-6124.

# THE SEARCH IS OVER FOR RESEARCH

Trying to instruct junior high and high school students in research skills is one of the most difficult tasks a secondary media specialist must face. Choosing, narrowing, and broadening topics are difficult concepts for students to grasp. If you're looking for a good search strategy, your search is now over! (Lifesaver Tool 93.1. Search Strategy Checklist Form)

## Lifesaver Tips

- This strategy provides a helpful way for students to gather information.

- Because many students tend to want to copy information directly from the encyclopedia, model how notes should be taken from the encyclopedia (i.e., substitution of words, change word order, etc.).

- If students cannot locate at least three books on the selected topic (or related topic), then another subject should be chosen.

- Because students have a difficult time with evaluating sources, talk about ways to tell if a source is helpful. For example, is the magazine article directly related to my subject? Are there at least three important facts I can use? These types of questions will help students make better choices about the materials they select.

- Remind students to find out the source of Internet information. For example, if the material came from a college or educational institution, it is bound to be more reliable than if it was authored by an unknown individual.

> ⟫ If you're searching for more time (aren't we all!), purchase the personal time management video (1-800-255-6139) and find out how you can gain two extra hours per day. When you have watched it, let teachers know the video is available.
>
> Pamela Bacon

# SEARCH STRATEGY CHECKLIST

**S**     SHARE possible topic with instructor. Approved? _____

Topic: _____

**E**     ENCYCLOPEDIA used: _____

List other closely related subjects found while browsing the encyclopedia:

1. _____

2. _____

3. _____

**A**     ADD three books to your encyclopedia article(s) (author last name, first name, title, place of publication, publisher, copyright date).

1. _____

2. _____

3. _____

**R**     REVIEW magazine articles on subject using *Readers' Guide* or online sources. Choose three related magazine articles (author last name, first name, title of article, title of magazine, date of magazine, pages).

1. _____

2. _____

3. _____

**C**     CHOOSE best three to five sources to use on research paper.

**H**     HIGHLIGHT or write notes on note cards.

**Lifesaver Tool 93.1.   Search Strategy Checklist Form**

# SEND STUDENTS' WORK "WRITE" AWAY!

Definitely one of the most time-consuming, but rewarding, jobs faced by teachers and media specialists alike is submitting students' writing to publishers. I can't give you more time, but I can give you a list of magazines that encourage and publish young authors. (Lifesaver Tool 94.1. Magazines That Publish Student Authors' Work)

## Lifesaver Tips

- Send for the writers guidelines of the magazine to which you plan to submit students' work (do this at least once a year because guidelines often change).

- Read guidelines thoroughly before submitting students' material.

- Send material for publication only if guidelines are met. There's no reason to waste their time (and yours!) if the submission will not even be considered.

- Create a form cover letter to submit with the student author's writing. The cover letter should include the following: student author's name, age, address, and telephone number. Also include the same information for yourself as sponsor (you can omit the age!). Be sure to state that the work is completely original and unpublished.

- Always send a self-addressed, stamped envelope.

- Make sure the envelope has enough postage for return of the material.

- Keep a copy of all outgoing correspondence in your files.

- Be patient! It can take months for a publisher to respond. The rule of thumb, though, is the longer it takes, the better your chances (rejection letters are usually received fairly quickly).

 America Online (AOL) has a section for budding young authors as part of their Writers Club. It's a great way for students to get the "write" idea! (http://www.aol.com/).

Pamela Bacon

# MAGAZINES THAT PUBLISH STUDENT AUTHORS' WORK

Amelia Student Award
c/o Amelia Magazine
329 E Street
Bakersfield, CA 93304

American Girl
830 Third Avenue
New York, NY 10022

Landmark Editions
P.O. Box 270169
Kansas City, MO 64127

Merlyn's Pen
P.O. Box 716
East Greenwich, RI 02818

Stone Soup
The Magazine by Young Writers
    and Artists
P.O. Box 83
Santa Cruz, CA 95063-0083

Young Playwrights, Inc.
Suite 906
321 W. 44th Street
New York, NY 10036

*Note*: For additional publications, please consult the latest edition of *The Writer's Market*.

**Lifesaver Tool 94.1.** **Magazines That Publish Student Authors' Work**

# PRACTICE YOUR POLICIES!

If the word *policy* makes you think of insurance, think of a library policy manual as an insurance plan for your library. A policy manual not only outlines library practices and procedures, it's also your insurance and protection against potential problems. (Lifesaver Tool 95.1. The DOs and DON'Ts of Policy Manuals)

## Lifesaver Tips

- If you don't have a policy manual now, form a team to share in the decision making and policy writing. Team members should include at least one teacher, parent, librarian, library aide, and administrator.

- If you have an outdated policy manual, form the same team to review the policy manual and update as needed.

- Before the writing process begins, obtain policy manuals from local schools. Having a good outline to follow will make the writing process easier.

- Write a draft of the manual with the team. Next, circulate the draft to solicit other feedback.

- When the final draft is written, have the original signed by the school board.

- Review the manual annually for possible changes and updates.

IIII➡  Be sure your policy manual includes a provision for the Internet. At our school, no student has access to the Internet without a signed parental permission slip on file.

Pamela Bacon

# THE DOs AND DON'Ts OF POLICY MANUALS

## DO INCLUDE

Mission statement/philosophy

Goals and objectives

Selection policy

Challenged materials policies

Processing procedures

Circulation procedures

Volunteer procedures

Student assistant procedures

Library aide selection, duties, and evaluation procedures

Library usage guidelines and procedures

Overdue policies

Media specialist job description and responsibilities

Weeding procedures

Procedures for accepting donated materials

## DON'T INCLUDE

Budget information

Inventory counts

Circulation counts

Names of helpers and volunteers

*Note*: All the above DON'Ts should be included in your annual report (Library Lifesaver 100) rather than in your library policy manual!

**Lifesaver Tool 95.1.   The DOs and DON'Ts of Policy Manuals**

From *100 Library Lifesavers.* © 1999 Libraries Unlimited. (800) 237-6124.

# CLIMB THE LADDER OF READING SUCCESS!

This idea has been a lifesaver because it monitors the skills mastered by my upper-elementary students. It's also easy to see at a glance where my students need a little extra boost. (Lifesaver Tool 96.1. Ladder of Reading Success)

## Lifesaver Tips

- This lifesaver is best used with grades 4–6.

- Photocopy forms and keep in class folders.

- When you check off all of the steps, send a note to the parent and the teacher acknowledging the child's success.

- Use a variety of tools (worksheets, learning centers, oral presentations, etc.) to measure the child's ability.

- For special-needs students, adjust the steps as needed.

- Make a display by posting a large ladder outside your media center. When students reach the top, post their names (or pictures!) on the ladder.

# LADDER OF READING SUCCESS

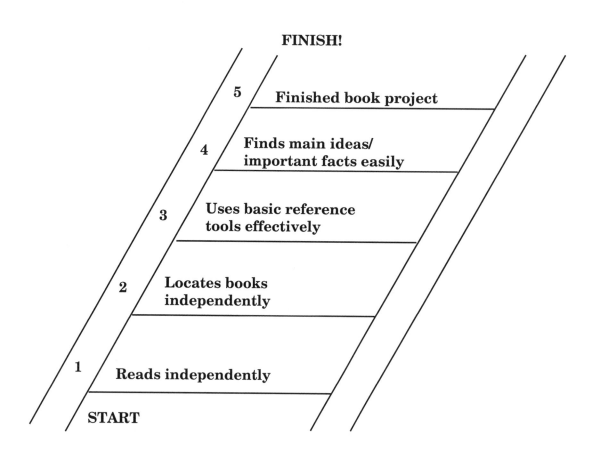

FINISH!

5  **Finished book project**

4  **Finds main ideas/ important facts easily**

3  **Uses basic reference tools effectively**

2  **Locates books independently**

1  **Reads independently**

**START**

From *100 Library Lifesavers.* © 1999 Libraries Unlimited. (800) 237-6124.

**Lifesaver Tool 96.1.   Ladder of Reading Success**

# LIBRARY LETTERS

The neat thing about this lifesaver is that it can be adapted to almost any grade level or subject area! (Lifesaver Tool 97.1. Lesson Plan for Library Letters) Students work in cooperative groups to spell out library- or book-related words. Can you spell *fun*?

## Lifesaver Tips

- Deduct points from groups who get too loud.

- Ask teachers for current vocabulary and spelling words to make classroom connections.

- Use any time you have a few extra minutes. Keep a running score. At the end of the year, award a small prize to the class with the highest points!

- Make each set of library letters on a different colored poster board. This prevents you from losing letters or from putting them in the wrong box.

- Try to find five large flat boxes of the same size and shape for library letter sets. If boxes are the same size, they stack and store more neatly.

---

 Store letters in bright, stackable Rubbermaid containers to prevent letters from escaping!

Pamela Bacon

---

# LESSON PLAN FOR LIBRARY LETTERS

Grade Levels: 2–8 (vary questions according to ability)

Objectives:
1. Students will practice spelling.

2. Students will gain proficiency in using library terms.

3. Students will work cooperatively in small groups.

Materials Needed:
Library Letters Game—one per group

Directions to Make Library Letters:
On a piece of poster board, print all the letters of the alphabet 10 times each with a dark marker. Laminate board. Cut apart letters and place them in a flat cardboard box.

Procedures:
1. Divide students in groups of four or five.

2. Place boxes of letters in the center of each table.

3. Tell students they will be "digging" for letters to form words.

4. The first group to spell the chosen word correctly gets a point.

5. Keep score on the chalkboard.

Examples of Questions:

Q: Who wrote *The Cat in the Hat*?
A: Students spell out the word *SEUSS*.

Q: What books are found in 796?
A: Students spell out the word *sports*.

As you can see, the possibilities for this activity are endless. Students enjoy this game and don't even realize they are learning important skills!

**Lifesaver Tool 97.1.    Lesson Plan for Library Letters**

# A PICTURE IS WORTH A THOUSAND WORDS

This lesson plan is truly one of the best I have ever used. I used the lesson in the English classroom for descriptive writing, then found it fit perfectly into a library lesson on periodicals! Hope it's a lifesaver for you, too! (Lifesaver Tool 98.1. A Picture Is Worth a Thousand Words)

## Lifesaver Tips

- Students should not show their pictures to any other student!

- This activity should take two library classes: the first one to browse through magazines, choose a picture, and write the descriptive paragraph; the second one to draw the picture described by another student.

- For best results, talk to classroom teachers before attempting this activity to make sure students have been exposed to descriptive writing!

- If a student has done a good job describing the picture in writing, the illustration should loosely match the original picture (regardless of the artistic ability of the student, believe it or not!).

- For behavior management, keep students at the same pace. If a student finishes writing early, he or she should silently read until everyone else is finished. Then go on to the illustration process.

IIII➡ Consider Subscription Services of America (1-516-679-8241) for your magazine renewals. They're efficient and economical.

Pamela Bacon

# A PICTURE IS WORTH A THOUSAND WORDS

## MAGAZINE ACTIVITY

Grade Level: upper-elementary/middle school

Objectives:
1.   Students will browse and become acquainted with new magazines.
2.   Students will practice descriptive writing.
3.   Students will draw a picture based on a descriptive paragraph.
4.   Students will use compare/contrast thinking skills to compare hand-drawn illustration with published picture.

Materials Needed:
lots of magazines (two or three per student)
pencils
writing paper
drawing paper
colored pencils

Procedures:
1.   Ask students to browse through magazines to locate a picture they believe they could describe in writing. (Obviously, you have final authority on pictures chosen!)
2.   After students choose their pictures, tell them to describe in writing everything they see in the picture.
3.   Students should include specific details such as sizes of objects, colors shown, objects in foreground, objects in background, any writing or captions, etc.
4.   When students finish their paragraphs, they should turn in their writing.
5.   Students then are given a paragraph written by another student to attempt to draw.

Culminating Activity:
At the end of the second library class (or beginning of the third), match the picture drawn with the original picture. It's fun to see how descriptive (or nondescriptive!) the writers were.

**Lifesaver Tool 98.1.   A Picture Is Worth a Thousand Words**

# ON A ROLL!

Whether you've been a media specialist for five minutes or five years, chances are, you know firsthand about the enormous amount of mail falling out of our already overflowing mailboxes. I think you'll find, as I have, that the rolling cart solution is a real lifesaver! (Lifesaver Tool 99.1. Get on a Roll)

## Lifesaver Tips

- Purchase a rolling cart with three baskets from an office supply store.

- Label the top (high priority) basket: "TO DO NOW."

- Label the middle (average/middle priority): "TO DO LATER."

- Label the bottom basket: "TO FILE."

- Begin by stacking mail into categories ( magazines, letters, packages, etc.).

- Use Post-it notes to mark down what the file items should be filed under. This step saves time later.

- Scan all material—don't bother reading items in their entirety that you will ultimately discard.

- Don't pile up mail to read when you have more time—read it and either toss it or put it in a basket. Deal with it now, not later.

- If you're not positive you want to purchase something, throw it away. With as much mail as we get, you can't save everything!

 To get on a roll, call LTD Commodities (1-847-295-5532). Their office organizer cart is only $14.95 and includes three rolling stack trays and removable side file bins.

Pamela Bacon

# GET ON A ROLL!

## MAIL ORGANIZATION METHOD

**R**  READ/REVIEW

Immediately open mail, read/review it, and act on it. Does it need to be put in the rolling basket or the wastebasket?

**O**  OUT

Throw out anything you don't absolutely need. I've learned the hard way that file cabinets only hold so much!

**L**  LOOK for and act on items that require immediate attention.

**L**  LEAVE it alone.

If it's something you want to save, but doesn't require immediate attention, put it in the file basket and let it go.

**Lifesaver Tool 99.1.**  **Get on a Roll**

# AN ANNUAL THING

I thought the last thing you do for the school year would be a fitting last lifesaver: the annual report. I believe a professionally done, well-thought-out annual report is an excellent communication tool to let administrators know what you're doing now and what you plan to do in the future. (Lifesaver Tool 100.1. Annual Report Checklist)

## Lifesaver Tips

- Before submitting your first annual report, find out from your principal or superintendent whether an annual report has been submitted in the past.

- If a report was submitted, ask for a copy to review.

- If a report was not submitted, brainstorm with your administrator a list of things he or she would like to see included in your report.

- Save a signed, dated copy in your file.

- Present a copy of your report to your building principal and carbon copy to the superintendent for reference. The superintendent may even wish to provide the school board with a copy.

- Have a trusted colleague review your report for typos or clarification. It's hard to see mistakes when you're not objective.

- Design a professional-looking cover.

- Enclose your report in a binder or report cover.

- An annual report can be an excellent data-driven tool to justify purchases or to make recommendations for change.

- Lifesaver Tool 100.2 (Annual Report Form) is a form that can be photocopied and typed on directly. Otherwise, the form can be typed into your computer and stored for each year's report.

⫸ Always save a copy of your annual report!

Pamela Bacon

# ANNUAL REPORT CHECKLIST

Before submitting your report, did you include

_____Circulation Reports

_____Library Usage Totals

_____Mission Statement

_____Goals (Reached and Future)

_____Library Assistant Evaluation

_____Library Volunteer/Student Helper Report

_____Teaming Schedule

_____New Materials Summary

_____Library Collection Summary

_____Strengths and Weaknesses of Library Program

_____Budget Totals and Information

**Lifesaver Tool 100.1.   Annual Report Checklist**

# ANNUAL REPORT FORM

I.  Background

II.  Mission Statement/Goals

III.  Circulation Reports

IV.  Library Usage Totals

V.  Library Collection/New Materials Summary

VI.  Strengths and Weaknesses (List three for each.)

VII.  Budget Ending Balances

VIII.  Library Assistant Evaluation

IX.  Student Assistant/Library Volunteer Report

X.  Teaming/Collaboration Efforts

XI.  Friends of the Library Club Report

**Lifesaver Tool 100.2.**   **Annual Report Form**

# BIBLIOGRAPHY

Anderson, Mary Alice. *Teaching Information Literacy Using Electronic Resources.* Worthington, OH: Linworth, 1996.

Andronik, Catherine. *School Library Management Notebook.* Worthington, OH: Linworth, 1994.

Avi. *Wolf Rider: A Tale of Terror.* New York: Aladdin Paperbacks, 1993.

Berry, Margaret A., and Patricia S. Morris. *Stepping into Research: A Complete Research Skills Activities Program for Grades 5–9.* New York: Center for Applied Research in Education, 1990.

Blanchard, Kenneth. *The One Minute Manager Meets the Monkey.* Austin, TX: Quill, 1991.

———. *The One Minute Manager.* New York: Berkley, 1993.

Coffin, M. T. *Don't Go to the Principal's Office.* New York: Camelot, 1996.

Conford, Ellen. *The Frog Princess of Pelham.* New York: Little, Brown, 1997.

Covey, Stephen R. *First Things First.* New York: Simon & Schuster, 1994.

Dolnick, Sandy. *Friends of the Libraries Sourcebook.* Chicago: American Library Association, 1996.

Farmer, Lesley S. J. *When Your Library Budget Is Almost Zero.* Englewood, CO: Libraries Unlimited, 1993.

*Free Stuff for Kids 1998.* Deephaven, MN: Meadowbook Press, 1997.

Hoffman, Jim. *Fabulous Principal Pie.* Grand Haven, MI: School Zone, 1993.

*Instant Art Notebook: An Easy Access Guide.* Worthington, OH: Linworth, 1992. (OOP*)

Jackson, Shirley. *The Lottery and Other Stories.* New York: Noonday Press, 1992.

Lewis, Marguerite, and P. Kudla. *Hooked on Library Skills: A Sequential Activities Program for Grades K–6.* New York: Center for Applied Research in Education, 1988.

Marra, Jean M. *Abridged Readers' Guide to Periodical Literature 1998.* New York: H. W. Wilson, 1998.

McMorrow, Catherine. *The Jellybean Principal.* New York: Random House, 1994.

Miller, Elizabeth B. *The Internet Resource Directory for K–12 Teachers and Librarians.* Englewood, CO: Libraries Unlimited, 1997.

Park, Barbara. *The Kid in the Red Jacket.* New York: Knopf, 1987.

*Self-Directing Library and Media Center Skills: An Easy Access Guide.* Troy, MO: Weber Costello. (OOP*)

Simpson, Carol Mann. *Copyright for School Libraries: A Practical Guide.* Worthington, OH: Linworth, 1994. (OOS*)

———. *Internet for Library Media Specialists.* Worthington, OH: Linworth, 1995.

Steinbeck, John. *The Grapes of Wrath.* Columbus, OH: Globe Fearon, 1996.

Streiff, Jane E. *Secondary School Librarian's Survival Guide.* New York: Center for Applied Research in Education, 1995.

Stripling, Barbara K., and Judy M. Pitts. *Brainstorms and Blueprints: Teaching Library Research as a Thinking Process.* Englewood, CO: Libraries Unlimited, 1988.

Sutton, Dave. *So You're Going to Run a Library: A Library Management Primer.* Englewood, CO: Libraries Unlimited, 1995.

*Tips and Other Bright Ideas for School Librarians.* Worthington, OH: Linworth, 1991.

Turner, Philip M., ed. *Helping Teachers Teach: A School Library Media Specialist's Role.* Englewood, CO: Libraries Unlimited, 1985.

Volkman, John D. *Cruising Through Research: Library Skills for Young Adults*. Englewood, CO: Libraries Unlimited, 1998.

White, E. B. *Charlotte's Web*. New York: Harper Trophy, 1974.

Wilder, Laura Ingalls. *Farmer Boy*. New York: Harper Trophy, 1973.

Williams, Constance D. *The Internet for Newbies: An Easy Access Guide*. Englewood, CO: Libraries Unlimited, 1997.

*World Almanac and Book of Facts*. Mahwah, NJ: World Almanac Press, 1998.

World Almanac Education. *How to Use an Almanac Kit*. Mahwah, NJ: World Almanac Press, 1995.

*The Writer's Market*. Cincinnati: F & W Publications, 1922. (Published annually.)

Wynar, Bohdan S., ed. *Recommended Reference Books for Small and Medium-sized Libraries and Media Centers*. Englewood, CO: Libraries Unlimited. (Published annually.)

---

*At this time, these books are out of stock (OOS) or out of print (OOP). Check with amazon.com about ordering these titles. This company is amazing at tracking down hard-to-get sources (http://www.amazon.com).

# INDEX